THE END OF PROGRESS

How Modern Economics Has Failed Us

THE END OF PROGRESS

How Modern Economics Has Failed Us

Graeme P. Maxton

John Wiley & Sons (Asia) Pte. Ltd.

Published in 2011 by John Wiley & Sons (Asia) Pte. Ltd.
1 Fusionopolis Walk, #07–01, Solaris South Tower, Singapore 138628

Other Wiley Editorial Offices
John Wiley & Sons, 111 River Street, Hoboken, NJ 07030, USA
John Wiley & Sons, The Atrium, Southern Gate, Chichester, West Sussex, P019 8SQ, United Kingdom
John Wiley & Sons (Canada) Ltd., 5353 Dundas Street West, Suite 400, Toronto, Ontario, M9B 6HB, Canada
John Wiley & Sons Australia Ltd., 42 McDougall Street, Milton, Queensland 4064, Australia
Wiley-VCH, Boschstrasse 12, D-69469 Weinheim, Germany

Library of Congress Cataloging-in-Publication Data
ISBN 978–0–470–82998–1 (Hardback)
ISBN 978–0–470–83000–0 (ePDF)
ISBN 978–0–470–82999–8 (Mobi)
ISBN 978–0–470–83001–7 (ePub)

Typeset in 11/14 Sabon Roman by MPS Limited, a Macmillan Company
Printed in Singapore by Markono Print Media Pte. Ltd.

10 9 8 7 6 5 4 3 2 1

Aufklärung ist der Ausgang des Menschen aus seiner selbstverschuldeten Unmündigkeit.
Enlightenment is how humanity can escape its self-inflicted immaturity.

Immanuel Kant

For my dear Bernice (aka Mitzi),
who was the inspiration for this book.

CONTENTS

ACKNOWLEDGMENTS

There are many people I want to thank, people who have made this book possible by influencing my life, ideas and path.

Andrea, Andrew, Arya, Alexina and Robin—all deserve special thanks. And those are just the people beginning with A (as well as one with R).

Andrea See has given me hard and soft(ware) support for as long as I have known her. Andrew Vine has promoted and encouraged me. He is a friend I couldn't do without. Arya K. Madanmohan, sometimes in New Delhi or London, has fed me ideas, wild and sane. Alexina and Robin Maxton are my strength.

I am grateful too, to Darrell Doren and Stephen Rocke in Hong Kong, as well as to many others who send me thoughts so regularly. I must also thank John Wormald in Chichester for his goodness and sagacity, for which I am eternally grateful. And Jay Kunkel, my brother in Shanghai or some airport, who is always so far ahead of the crowd with his observations and views. Maria Hovdar in Eugendorf too, for her immense wisdom, compassion for others, understanding of humanity and vision. *Auch für Ihre Geduld und jedes Frühstück bei Kerzenschein.* Nor would this book have been as it is without the good advice and support of Nick Melchior.

For the past, I must gratefully acknowledge and thank James and Jimmy Maxton for their enlightened genes.

Graeme Maxton
Singapore, 2011

1

IT'S ABOUT YOU—YOU ARE RESPONSIBLE TOO

No society can be flourishing and happy, of which the far greater part of the members are poor and miserable.

Adam Smith

We should all feel a sense of embarrassment. Humanity has finally evolved to a point where our species is moving backwards. We are destroying more than we build. Every year the world economy grows by about $1.5 trillion (or a thousand billion). But, every year, we devastate the planet to the tune of $4.5 trillion.[1] We have officially moved into reverse, laying waste to more than we create.

Even so, most of us have grown sanguine about such statistics.

We all know that humankind has some problems. But then, there are bound to be difficult consequences for the planet when there are seven billion people in the world. So many of us ignore those and comfort ourselves instead by focusing on the counter-balancing evidence of our progress.

We have certainly achieved much in recent decades. More people enjoy more freedom and opportunity today than at any time in history. Life expectancies and standards of nutrition are higher in most parts of the world than ever before. There is more openness for trade between peoples. We have benefited from some of the fastest, most sustained economic growth for generations.

More people are educated to a higher level than in the past, and millions have been lifted out of absolute poverty. Women's rights have dramatically improved in many parts of the world and are now far removed from where they once were. Human rights are stronger too, with slavery mostly abolished, and the right to say, do and act as you will, greatly improved in almost all countries during the last thirty years.

The environmental damage we are causing is worrying, of course, especially when it is changing the climate. But what else can we expect? Transforming the planet is a consequence of our development. Pollution, deforestation and blighted landscapes from resource extraction are some of the negative effects of humankind's progress.

Moreover, a great deal of the destruction we have wrought is likely to be short-lived. Look at Europe. Much of the continent was once covered by forests. Yet their destruction hundreds of years ago had little effect on the world. More recently, coal-fired homes and factories in the United Kingdom (UK) created an air so toxic that it shortened the lives of millions. But we learned how to solve that problem and the air quality is now better. Or look at the United States (US). Some of its rivers were once dead, completely without life, because of industrial effluent. But they recovered. And, while humankind may be killing off thousands of species, we don't seem to be suffering any ill effects. We did not need the dodo. Why are tigers any different?

As for resource extraction, what else can we do? We need raw materials for growth. We cannot progress without digging metals and fossil fuels out of the earth. To stop would be to deny most people on the planet the chance to get rich, the chance to live in healthy modern societies. Reducing the pace with which we dig for coal or mine for oil would condemn billions to poverty for longer. Besides, by the time the oil has gone we will have developed a replacement, a hydrogen- or solar-based society, which is entirely pollution free. Invention is the nature of humankind.

Similarly, we know that there are food and water shortages in many parts of the world. More than one billion people live without enough to eat. But we can surely solve this problem too. Let's not get carried away by the ideas of the Reverend Malthus, and his gloomy predictions of global famines because of insufficient food. He was wrong 200 years ago and he is wrong today. We can genetically engineer better crops, improve yields and desalinate the seas.

Yes, we are destroying more than we create. It is a consequence of our existence. We will find an answer. Just as we always have, won't we?

Unfortunately, planetary destruction is not humankind's only big challenge.

We have huge financial worries. Because of the economic crisis in the US and Europe in 2007, many of the world's largest economies are bust, laden with debts so large they cannot be repaid. Despite trillions of dollars of emergency support, the global economy remains dangerously unstable, with a bumpy path ahead.

Socially, there are signs of trouble brewing. Financial inequality is rising. The gap between rich and poor is wider today in most of the world than for decades. In the US it is wider than it was in the 1920s. Billions of people around the world are becoming fatter and less healthy. In much of the developed world, standards of education are falling.

Fundamental democratic ideas are also being corrupted. Many of our politicians seem to be mostly motivated by profit and the thrill of being in power. Few voice a desire to bring us a better life and give us hope for the future; few encourage us to raise our sights. There is little moral or social ideology behind their chat-show rhetoric and newscast sound-bites. As a result, millions of voters throughout the West have become bored and apathetic, uninterested in the systems that make our world tick, caring little about the principles at stake. We have even returned to an age where we fight wars about religion, just as we did hundreds of years ago.

More worrying still, the pillars of liberty are under assault too. With so much snooping by governments of many countries in the name of security, we are steadily undermining long-preserved notions of freedom.

Most troubling of all, few real solutions are being proposed to these problems. There is airy hope, a belief, that many of these difficulties are simply necessary for now; that it will be all right in the end; that humankind's innovativeness will somehow come to the rescue. We will find a replacement for the world's oil when it is gone. We will somehow pay back all the debts. We will invent new ways to feed the world. We will restore hard-won legal rights when the war on terror is over.

There is, however, little substance behind these thoughts. We lack a clear plan or timetable to address the multitude of issues we face. Instead of focusing on material progress, we think instead about material gains.

Most critically, we are ignoring one vital element: many of these troubles are closely interlinked; they have the same cause. The resource shortages, the financial troubles, the political and social problems are all the result of changes we have made to the way we think about our world. And almost all of these changes have happened in the last thirty years. We have abandoned many long-cherished ideas, almost without noticing.

The environmental destruction, debts and food shortages are the price.

To understand what is happening and why, we need to go back more than 200 years to the time of the Enlightenment. We need to return to the theories of Adam Smith, the father of modern economics and one of that age's greatest champions. His ideas about the free market and the "invisible hand" lie at the heart of most Western societies, as well as many others. They are at the core of our economic world. They are also at the center of almost all of our problems.

During the last thirty years, we have taken many of Smith's principles and trashed them. We have invented, instead, a new and distorted set of ideas with which to run our world: these are the source of many of our difficulties.

Since the late 1970s, wily politicians and wooly-headed academics have persuaded us to forget many of the ideas that lie at the foundations of Smith's theories. We have been encouraged instead to cling to the labels he used, without really understanding their meaning. We have warped his ideas, as well as other enlightenment principles—including those of democracy, social responsibility and justice—to suit our own ends. We use the same words as enlightenment thinkers, but our understanding of what these words mean has changed. Like mutated genes, we have found meanings far removed from the original intent.

Smith's principles were about more than economics; they were about more than the free market and the invisible hand. In many ways his thoughts and opinions embodied the whole of the Enlightenment age.

The Enlightenment was a time of dramatic intellectual, social and political progress. It took place in the eighteenth and early nineteenth centuries, mainly in Europe and America. Influenced by the American and French Revolutions, it encouraged people to think that they could challenge convention and question authority. As one of the foremost thinkers of the time, Immanuel Kant, put it, the Enlightenment was "daring to know."

The Enlightenment brought us modern science. It brought us reasoning. After the centuries when the Western world had been dominated by the church, the monarchy and superstition, it encouraged and stimulated discussion about the meaning of personal freedom and democracy. Notions about republicanism led to the Declaration of Independence in America. Enlightenment ideas were the source of later concepts concerning liberalism, sexual equality, meritocracy and the right to privacy. The Enlightenment was a seed bed, planted with new ideas that grew to create a giant forest of thoughts, sustaining us for generations.

The Enlightenment was about more than ideas though. It was about transforming values, with the opportunities for improvement open to everyone. It led to reforms in education and to the establishment of libraries where people could access books: magazines, journals and public lectures encouraged debate. In France, a thirty-five-volume encyclopedia was published with the aim of changing the way people thought. With more than 70,000 articles written by some of the foremost thinkers of the time, the books were an attempt to refresh the minds of citizens about their purpose, their world and their lives. Their authors aimed to destroy superstition through reason and give everyone access to scientific knowledge and modern ideas.

It is hard to overstate the importance of the shift in thinking that the Enlightenment brought. It is the foundation of almost all modern Western political and intellectual culture.

It was within this world that Smith developed his ideas. The foundations for his theories lay not in economics but in moral philosophy. In all his thinking there were principles of justice, tolerance and fairness that needed to be upheld.

During the last three decades we have banished many of these principles to the fringes, or trampled them underfoot. We have abandoned many of Smith's core beliefs. We have demoted notions of justice and fairness, promoting instead simplified ideas of individuality and unrestrained market freedom.

Such changes are behind the financial crisis in the US and Europe in 2007 and are the reason many of our societies are increasingly divided. Modern economic thinking has led us to under-value our world, accelerating the pace of planetary destruction. We mine lands to fuel factories, to power cars and illuminate homes. But we price the world's resources at the cost of their extraction plus a share for some profit, and no more. We ignore the costs that will be incurred by future generations when the resources are gone, or the environmental damage we cause by digging them up and using them. We use the world's raw materials on the cheap, leaving others to pay much of the cost. We think primarily about short-term profit and less about long-term social gain. This does not reflect the ideas of Smith. It does not follow his principles of economics.

Such wrong-headedness has also allowed other Enlightenment principles to fade.

Instead of raising the sights and ambitions of our peoples, as the French encyclopedia tried to do, we have allowed a cult of celebrity, a hunger for pointless brands, and a belief that information is knowledge to constrain our thinking. By ignoring Smith's ideas about social fairness, we have dismissed widening income inequalities as if they do not matter. Yet they are unsustainable and dangerous, the stuff of revolution.

Unless we take a different path, we will have to wave goodbye to social order but will be able to welcome instead an age of lesser plenty, of fewer rights and greater conflict.

Unless we cease squandering our most precious resources, many poor countries will never be able to industrialize. They will be plundered of the means to develop by China and the West: their oil reserves sucked dry, their forests gone and their coal seams scraped clean. No amount of innovativeness or human ingenuity can replace many of the world's resources when they are gone. Optimistic modern-day economists need to have a chat with their colleagues who study the hard sciences if they are in any doubt. There are laws in the world of physics and chemistry, and unlike those of economics, they do not change. We cannot simply manufacture new supplies of copper, zinc or oil when the existing ones have gone.

Modern economic thinking has given us false goals, demanding growth for its own sake, encouraging a mania for consumption that requires the planet to be laid waste, exploited for our convenience.

In return, we were persuaded that progress would come along for the ride. We have experienced fast economic growth, for sure. But we have also created a world that is unstable. In many places, for the first time in centuries, we face falling life expectancies. We risk battles about food, water and oil as resources decline. We face strife over political ideologies and the rise of nationalism.

We were persuaded that there were no limits to growth. We thought we did not have to care about the consequences of our actions. We believed that the responsibility to borrow money within our limits, or the obligation to use the world's resources considerately was for others.

As we are about to learn, that was wrong.

Endnote

1. The Economics of Ecosystems and Biodiversity (TEEB), "Mainstreaming the Economics of Nature": a synthesis of the approach, conclusions and recommendations of TEEB, October 20, 2010. US Census Bureau.

Part 1

Our Belief in the Free Market Failed Us

2

TOO MUCH CHOICE, TOO LITTLE RESTRAINT

Economics is extremely useful as a form of employment for economists.

John Kenneth Galbraith, economist

Fetch the Tool Box

A major cause of our problems is modern economic thinking.

The pillars of the Western economic system were mostly established in the eighteenth century. They are based on the work of many economists and philosophers at the time, the best known of whom was Adam Smith. The ideas contained in his famous book, *An Inquiry into the Nature and Causes of the Wealth of Nations,* are still at the heart of much economic theory today.

In practice, however, many modern economic theories have lost touch with Smith's most cherished principles. Modern-day economists talk blithely about Smith and his ideas as if their subject adheres strongly to his theories. But it does not, and in several important ways.

Smith is best known for the notion of the invisible hand, although this was not his idea originally and it was first mentioned in his previous book, *The Theory of Moral Sentiments.*

Today, the invisible hand is a popular metaphor for free markets and a *laissez-faire*[1] economic philosophy: trade should be largely unrestricted and markets should be lightly regulated. But the way we understand these ideas today is not the way Smith intended them.

Smith was first a professor of logic and then of moral philosophy and his principles of economics were derived from his work in these subjects. They rested heavily on ideas of efficiency, balance and social justice. Although Smith strongly advocated free competition and open trade, as well as a minimum level of government interference, he also saw fairness as vital to all economic activities.

For there to be a social balance, for example, Smith believed that the rich should be taxed more than the poor.[2] Although he saw politics as wholly separate from economics, he also argued that sometimes governments needed to take steps to ensure no one exercised too much power in the market.

The "wealth" mentioned in the title of *The Wealth of Nations* was not monetary wealth. His book is not about how countries can get rich. It is about how they can improve the well-being of their ordinary citizens. He believed economics was about how society could achieve prosperity and progress. It was also about achieving fairness and justice.

Although he talked about individuals acting in their own "self interest," it was not understood then as it is today. The actual term he used was "rational self interest," and it was not about acting selfishly, it was about acting responsibly, with a sense of duty to others. Smith believed that there is a powerful sense within all of us to help our fellow men and women, not to hurt or exploit them:

> How selfish soever man may be supposed, there are evidently some principles in his nature, which interest him in the fortune of others, and render their happiness necessary to him, though he derives nothing from it except the pleasure of seeing it.[3]
>
> ADAM SMITH

Each of us should act freely, Smith said, guided by the invisible hand and in the interests of social harmony.

Smith's enlightened underlying ideas about social responsibility remained vital elements of Western economic thought for many years. While some of his principles were gradually diluted and others sometimes ignored, such as those on the need to regulate monopolies, the basic moral pillars remained unchanged during almost all of the nineteenth century.

In the years following World War I, however, there was a widespread belief in the need for radical social and political change. There was a desperate need for new investment too, to encourage recovery and, it was hoped, create a better world. New discoveries seemed to offer the tantalizing possibility of an entirely different kind of society, a new paradigm, where war and poverty could be banished forever. Investors, spurred by rising stock markets, believed in an upward and self-sustaining spiral of progress and rising wealth. But the unleashed flurry of greed which followed also led to a vast speculative bubble and the Great Crash of 1929.

In the fall out, politicians recognized that markets left to their own devices can often get things wrong. So, over the following years, politicians began to take a much larger role in defining economic policies. Governments around the world believed that they needed to carefully regulate the banks and stock market companies, which they saw as being largely responsible for the "crash."

With the growing power of trade unions and the influence of new political ideas, some countries even nationalized many of their primary industries—coal, electricity generation, gas supply, media, steel, telecoms and water. The politicians and economists of the time believed that these businesses would benefit from state control. The coal and power generation industries needed heavy investment and provided products or services for all citizens. Under state control, went the thinking, no individual could extract unfair profits from a country's natural resources. Other industries were regarded as strategic, like telecoms or state media businesses. These needed close supervision to make sure they acted in society's best interests.

Economists of the time believed that the invisible hand had caused the 1929 bubble, at least partly. They concluded that it needed to be guided, that markets should be regulated by governments.

By the late 1970s, however, many of the drawbacks of state control had become obvious. There were frequent strikes in many countries, with workers accused of holding their governments to ransom. State-owned companies were now seen as inefficient and bureaucratic, partly because they had no competitors.

This led to a radical change in thinking, which, in some ways, took the Western world back to the ideas that had been popular during the 1920s. A new wave of economists, notably those from the Chicago School in America, began forcibly to argue for a more hands-off approach. They believed that government intervention was best kept to a minimum and that markets should be given more freedom to police themselves.

A new sort of politician appeared at the same time. In the US, Ronald Reagan was elected to the White House, while Margaret Thatcher became Prime Minister in Britain. Thatcher, in particular, inherited a country that was riven by labor problems.

Both politicians had a strong belief that the influence of the state on enterprise was inefficient and bureaucratic, that it represented a "dead hand" on the levers of growth and progress. US politicians were also keen to prove that their model of economic development was superior to that of their Cold War enemies at the time. The free market could triumph over the Soviet system, dominated as it was by government ownership.

So emerged the Washington consensus; a group of economists, politicians and journalists who argued for less government involvement and more freedom for the market. Global institutions such as the International Monetary Fund (IMF) and the World Bank joined the chorus. And all of them provided a renewed sense of energy to US foreign policy, which encouraged other countries to adopt the American model of democracy and freedom, with liberalized, deregulated markets.

The change in thinking was also driven partly by opportunity. The banking sector was seen as being stifled in the decades following the Great Crash of 1929 and the ensuing Depression. The tight regulatory controls that had been introduced to constrain its activities had divided investment banks from retail banks. This had limited their ability to speculate, grow and offer new financial products. Modern economic thinking allowed bankers to argue that these restrictive controls should now be lifted.

Soon the mantra became: "the markets are always right, governments are always wrong."[4] Gradually, the cry for free markets, free trade and individual choice was heard around the world. Politicians in the US, the UK, Australia, Ireland, as well as parts of Asia, were especially keen to hear the new call and adopted the ideas readily. Much of the European Union was less enthusiastic. It did not follow this path so unquestioningly, preferring to keep a much greater level of state involvement instead.

But the new ideas certainly seemed to work. The following thirty years saw the fastest period of world economic growth ever. More liberalized internal markets, globalization and the gradual opening up of countries like China and India brought unprecedented new opportunities. The banking sector grew especially quickly.

But the power unleashed by the largely unrestricted free-market mantra also brought more volatility. Economies and prices were more prone to bubbles, such as the information technology boom in the late 1990s and the sharp rises in food and commodity prices nearly a decade later. Speculation was not only tolerated but encouraged, allowing the prices of many items to become divorced from the real level of underlying demand. Consumer spending also rose rapidly, with much of it fueled by debt. Income inequalities widened.

Eventually, of course, the under-regulated free-market model led to a massive financial bubble. The system failed, just as it had in the 1920s. The largest debt bubble in history led to the 2007 financial crisis and the biggest bank bailout ever.

That this bubble had been created should not have come as a surprise. It should not have been a shock to anyone that a complex system, left unregulated, had got badly out of control. Politicians, government officials and economists should have known that this would happen—just as it had before. They should have seen that allowing people to borrow too much was neither sustainable nor socially responsible. They should have known that giving bankers too much freedom would lead to trouble—because it always had in the past. Legislators should have punctured the bubble before it got too big. They had a duty to society, a duty of care.

Indeed, all of us, as consumers, citizens and voters, should have seen that something was wrong. The rise in wealth and pace of growth were not natural and we knew it. But most of us chose instead the path of blindness, of personal short-term gain rather than long-term social responsibility.

Economics Is Not Rocket Science: It Is Not Even Science

The West's politicians and regulators should have known that what they were being told was wrong. They should have known that economics was never intended to provide an all-encompassing, self-regulatory, model of social progress. Along with the regulators, they should have known that economics is not a science, despite being labeled that way, and despite the claims of many academics and economists who wish that it was.

This distinction is important. Modern-day economists like to talk about the laws of economics because they want all of us to see their subject as one with hard-and-fast rules. They want us to think that there are economic certainties. They want to be seen as clever, trusted experts with their mastery of complex concepts and baffling theories. For thirty years, they told Western governments to let the market allocate resources, set prices and ensure supply met demand. Smith's invisible hand would ensure that the system was self regulating, they said. Governments should interfere as little as possible.

Yet this was only a theory and for the second time in a century it failed.

Economics is not a science like physics or chemistry, where experiments and observations produce consistent results. It is not a subject where predictions can be made with much certainty. If we heat two chemicals together we know what the outcome will be. If we repeat the process we will get the same result. Economics does not work like this. If a government cuts interest rates or raises taxes, economists do not actually know what will happen. If the government does it a second time, economists cannot, even then, predict accurately what will happen based on what happened before. The results are often different from those expected.

Economists say this is because there are often too many "variables." They like to blame "externalities," which are variables that were not obvious at the time. Yet these externalities can be critically important.

An externality of burning fossil fuels is that it pollutes the atmosphere. This causes respiratory problems as well as many other diseases and is one of the causes of climate change. But because these consequences are seen as externalities, economists failed to quantify the effects. As a result, the costs were largely ignored for years. This led to what Lord Stern, who headed the UK's study on climate change, called "the greatest failure of the market the world has ever seen."[5]

Because politicians and regulators believed unquestioningly in the economists and their airy faith in the power of the market, much of the world was lured into thinking that burning fossil fuels had few consequences. It caused a bit of smog, some breathing difficulties, and polluted the planet a bit. But we were persuaded that these troubles came without a cost. We ignored the wider consequences, dismissing them as externalities.

Even today, we continue to ignore many of the costs that arise from our use of fossil fuels. The price we pay for oil, gas and coal does not reflect the environmental damage these fuels cause. It does not account for their steady depletion or the implications of this for future generations.

Modern economic thinking encourages us to price the world's natural resources incorrectly. It allows us to use them on the cheap, ignoring many of the costs. As we will see later, similar wrong-headedness is also the cause of our mania for consumption. It is even responsible for us having too many children.

How Has Economics Failed Us? Let Me Count the Ways

Economics is not all bunkum of course. Many of Smith's ideas are still as valid today as they were when first put forward. But the charge sheet of what is wrong with modern economic thinking is nonetheless extensive.

Modern economics supports free trade even when it is not beneficial to both sides. It encourages excess choice, to the detriment of the planet and our societies. It widens social divisions. And it encourages growth for its own sake.

Smith was a famous advocate of free trade. But trade should not be entirely unrestricted. Free trade does not work when one country has nothing to sell or is exploited. It does not always work with strategic industries, which sometimes need protection, or for businesses that take time to grow. Trade should be as free as possible, but it should not be wholly uncontrolled.

Overly liberalized markets make it impossible for developing countries to industrialize. Modern thinking on trade suggests that developing countries should sell their resources to industrialized countries and get complex manufactured goods in return. Developing countries can provide their coal in return for cars and DVD players. Rich countries get the resources they need and a market where they can sell their produce. Poor countries can sell their resources and get fancy first-world products in return.

But what if developing countries want to make cars and DVD players themselves? What if they want to build societies based on more than mining, drilling and logging? What if they want to provide jobs to locally educated scientists and engineers? With unrestricted free trade, establishing their own industrial foundations is almost impossible. If they try to build industries they will face resistance from companies in developed countries anxious to prevent the rise of new competitors.

Companies in developing countries cannot compete if there is unrestricted free trade. Without economies of scale or experience, they are unable to make the cars and DVD players as cheaply as rivals in industrialized countries. Nor can they develop their own competitive technologies. Their locally developed products cost more than imported ones. Consequently, unrestricted free trade makes it almost impossible for developing countries to industrialize.

If trade between rich and poor countries is fully liberalized, a developing country has to accept that it will always be a developing country. Either that, or it has to introduce restrictions to trade. With trade barriers in place it can establish an industrial base, have citizens pay more for the locally made cars and DVD players for a while, encounter the wrath of foreign partners, and then open its borders when it is able to compete.

This is what China has been doing for the last twenty-five years. China does not believe in unrestricted free trade—which makes sense from a social point of view and from a developmental point of view. Trade barriers allow it to develop. But such policies do not fit with the laws of modern Western economics. So Western countries accuse China of cheating and acting unfairly.

It is wrong simply to say that free trade is good and that closed markets are bad. Yet that is what modern Western economics has encouraged us to think.

A DVD Player Should Cost More than Lunch

Modern economic thinking has also mispriced our world. It has failed to put a value on pollution, waste and the disposal costs of many items we use. It has encouraged us to think about the short term, not the needs of future generations.

The price we pay for our resources has almost nothing to do with what they are worth. It is madness that a barrel of oil, which took millions of years of planetary activity to create, which comes from a declining reserve, and which could be of value to many generations to come, is worth $150 or less. That price encourages us to waste it—as we do. More then 80 percent of it is squandered. Nor does the price reflect the pollution it causes, the greenhouse gases it releases, or the environmental damage caused during its extraction.

Similarly, water is a finite resource, essential to our existence. Yet throughout much of the world it is used wastefully because it is free. Factories and ships are allowed to pollute rivers and seas without any consequences, while hundreds of millions of people live without enough food because there is not enough water to irrigate their fields.

In the same way, we destroy the rainforests and overfish the oceans. We kill off species by the thousands without apparent cost—because today's sort of economics does not provide us with a practical means to value them. Because we are so unwilling to regulate markets most of the legislation introduced to stop these abuses fails. It does not fail because what we are doing to the oceans and the planet is unimportant, or has no cost.

The price of our disregard for nature is hardly ever reflected in the cost of the items we buy—although it should be, according to classical economic theory.

When we buy soap that uses palm oil the price does not reflect the value of the rainforests that were burned to grow the oil palm trees. It does not account for the death of the species that once lived in the forest, often burned alive when it was destroyed. Nor does it pay for the speed with which oil palm trees expend the remaining nutrients in the soil. When we eat fish there is no direct cost associated with acquiring them from the seas. We simply pay the indirect cost of having fishermen take boats out into the oceans to empty them of fish. The oceans are not paid.

In much of the world it costs more to hire a bicycle than a car, despite the difference in resources needed to manufacture each of them and their respective environmental costs. A DVD player is cheaper than lunch in an average Western restaurant even though the lunch uses ingredients that can be replaced while the DVD player does not. A flight from London to Athens often costs less than the bus ride to the airport. A pair of glasses costs more than a washing machine. The price of a 100 mile journey by car is less than the price of taking the train, despite the higher costs in terms of pollution, congestion and land use. Hotels charge more to wash a pair of socks than it costs to replace them.

Modern economic thinking has created these pricing anomalies. Across the world, items are being under-valued while others are being thrown away unnecessarily because it is cheaper than reusing them. This makes no sense from an environmental standpoint, or a moral one.

We will explore the reasons behind these anomalies later.

For Richer and Poorer

For some of us, of course, modern economic theories have paid dividends. The unleashed power of the market, the mispricing of the world's resources and the consumerism these have spawned, mean some people have become much richer—and possibly even happier. While in the past, their gains may have been matched by a greater sense of social responsibility, a duty to those less fortunate, today's richest citizens are largely free from such moral shackles.

And the wealthy remain the minority. For most people in the world, modern economics has brought them nothing much at all. Although millions of people were lifted from absolute poverty in the last fifteen years, the improvement in their lives did not last for long. The financial crisis and rising food prices have shoved many of them right back where they started. Even in the developed world many of the rewards of the free-market system look more like penalties; a mountain of debt, the rise of undependable low-grade employment and widespread obesity.

Even modern-day economists tell us that this was not meant to happen. The free market was supposed to distribute wealth more evenly. The wealth was meant to gradually trickle down. The rich would spend their money and, through some unspecified process, this would eventually reach the bottom of the pyramid, enriching the poor.

It has not happened. Instead, the gap between rich and poor has grown in almost every country on earth during the last thirty years.

This is bad news for everyone. Studies show, consistently, that societies with low levels of income inequality are less violent, healthier and more trusting. It is no coincidence that America's boom decades, during the 1950s and 1960s, were at a time when income inequality was at its lowest level for decades. Nor is it simple chance that Japan remained socially stable during more than twenty years of stagnation. It was partly down to keeping the gap between rich and poor very narrow. Limiting the wealth divide between rich and poor even raises average life expectancies.

Of course, some degree of income inequality is useful, desirable even. Individual effort should be rewarded. We are not all the same. But the huge differences that exist in the US, much of Latin America, Asia and Africa today, are counter-productive and damaging. They are a threat to social cohesion.

As we will see in the coming chapters, however, it is not the only threat.

Endnotes

1. Meaning, to let or allow, to take a hands-off approach.
2. "It is not very unreasonable that the rich should contribute to the public expense, not only in proportion to their revenue, but something more than in that proportion," *An Enquiry into the Nature and Causes of the Wealth of Nations*, (Book 5, Chapter 2, Article 1).
3. *From The Theory of Moral Sentiments*, 1759, Part I, Section I, Chapter I.
4. OECD Road to Recovery Forum, "Future of Capitalism," May 2010, Paris.
5. Stern Review on the Economics of Climate Change, October 30 2006.

3

A BROKEN FINANCIAL SYSTEM

If money be not thy servant, it will be thy master.

Sir Francis Bacon

Consumption, Not Love, Was the Drug

It may not be the most important consequence of thirty years of weak economic thinking but it is certainly the most obvious. And although we might prefer to see it as an event from the past, something we would rather consign to memory, the 2007 financial crisis was much more serious than that. Like the radiation which lingers after a nuclear explosion, Western economies will glow in the fallout for years.

The radioactivity that remains is debt—consumer debt, bank debt and government debt—and it will constrain our world with its dark shadow for a long time to come.

The world economy was and remains largely dependent on consumption; on all of us buying the items we need to live every day. Because they have the biggest economies, this means it is mostly dependent on Western consumption. In the US, more than 70 percent of economic activity comes from people buying cars and cameras, flat-pack furniture, underpants and shoes. In Germany, where consumers have a reputation for being more frugal, consumption still accounts for 60 percent of the economy.

Consumption also accounts for a large proportion of many developing economies. But because spending per head is so much smaller, the overall value is less significant. It is Western consumption that has been the fuel of the global economy. It is Western consumption that has driven the world's economic growth during the last thirty years.

For the world economy to expand, Western societies needed to keep consuming more. And to consume more meant at least one of two factors needed to keep changing: either consumers had to find more money to spend, or the costs of what they bought needed to keep falling. Both happened and both were the result of the change in economic thinking that took place in the late 1970s.

Manufacturers around the world worked tirelessly to drive down the price of almost everything they made. In real terms, a car, washing machine and pair of shoes cost much less in 2010 than they did in 1980, on a like-for-like basis.

To achieve this, businesses cut costs. They relocated factories to developing countries, like China or Bangladesh, to reduce wages. They redesigned their products to make them easier to assemble and ship. They drove down the prices they paid for components and raw materials. Governments signed free-trade deals to support them, opening up markets, cutting red tape, and reducing the costs of shipping goods around the world.

These actions helped make the world "flatter," making it cheaper to move toys and tinsel manufactured in Tianjin to markets in Toronto, Tokyo and Tel Aviv.

This was globalization.

While this drive to cut costs and boost sales may have seemed laudable at the time, many people learned that there were unpleasant side effects. Jobs were lost as factories in North America and Europe closed. Workers in Indonesia and China, some of them children, were often exploited; forced to work long hours on low pay. In much of the developing world, factory waste was pumped into rivers, unregulated, killing life downstream. Forests were bulldozed. Governments made dubious arrangements to secure fuel supplies and win access to natural resources. And the quality of many goods fell: they were designed to break, become obsolete or become unfashionable quickly, because this encouraged even more consumption.

At the same time, Western consumers found new ways to spend. Although real incomes barely improved throughout this time, particularly in the US, consumers started to dig into their savings. They also began to borrow more, even taking out loans against their homes.

These loans were mostly provided by banks, credit card and finance companies. The bankers were delighted to lend, not just to make a profit but because politicians, economists and regulators were encouraging them. All of them feared, rightly, that the economic growth would slow if they did not. Without more borrowing there would be less consumption and the factories would not be able to expand. The ships and the air-freight companies would have to idle their container terminals and airplanes. The entire economic engine would stall.

No one wanted that.

It was this thirty-year consumption and borrowing mania that led to the financial crisis in 2007. That this happened is largely the responsibility of modern-day economists. They were the source of the notion that markets should be minimally regulated. They encouraged politicians and regulators to step back and let the invisible hand do most of the work. They were responsible for the world adopting the strategy of the cancer cell, for leading us to believe that growth should be a purpose and not an outcome. They were the source of policies that encouraged banks to lend without restraint and allowed people to borrow more than they should.

The reason the effects of this crisis will linger for so long is because of the level of debt that remains. In the US and much of Europe consumer and bank debts are larger than the economies. Banks around the world remain crippled by millions of worthless loans. After 2007, to bail out the banks, governments also took on more debt than they should.

Like the morning after the night before, the developed world now has to deal with a financial hangover that has come from thirty years of over-indulgence.

How big is the world?

When it comes to the world's debt and the size of banks we need to talk in trillions. When numbers get that large, most of us get a bit lost in all the digits. So, what is a trillion? A trillion is a thousand billion. It is 1 with 12 zeros after it. A trillion dollars is equal to the sales of Wal-Mart in two and a half years. All the economic value created in the world each year added up to around $60 trillion in 2009. The GDP of India, or Russia, or the State of Texas was just over $1 trillion in 2009. The GDP of America was $14 trillion. In China and Japan it was $5 trillion and Germany $3.4 trillion. The economic activity of Switzerland, Indonesia or Belgium was roughly half a trillion dollars in 2009. America's debts were more than $80 trillion.

How Far Is Down?

The tale of financial woe, which is a result of the developed world's thirty-year consumption party, comes in three parts. Unfortunately none have happy endings.

The first part concerns consumer debt in the US and much of Europe. Without some debt forgiveness and a lot of time, millions of those who bought too many iPods, pullovers and kitchens, could face bankruptcy.

The second part is about the banking system. Weak regulation and thirty years of irresponsible lending mean that much of the world's financial system remains a liability. How we can deal with this hangover is not obvious or easy.

The third part is about government debt in the West and in Japan. Because of bank bail outs, and emergency economic support measures, this has risen rapidly. Government debt will also continue to grow for some time to come and, at some point, this will need to be repaid. Yet for some governments this will be impossible. The debts will be too high, and the interest—and hence repayments—too great to prevent the debts getting higher still. Some governments in the developed world will have to default. Therein lies the problem.

While the financial crisis in 2007 may have seemed like an earthquake at the time, it was only a taster of what will come unless the West faces up to its financial problems. What happened in 2007 was not a correction. It was just a crack in the Western financial system, like having a wobbly leg on a table.

Unfortunately, despite several banks having gone bust, the West still faces the biggest debt bubble in history—and it will have implications for decades.

Critically, it is very unlikely that modern economists, government regulators and the free market will be able to fix these troubles. They were the cause of them. To get out of the financial hole the West's spending mania has caused will require radical measures and a different way of thinking.

Consumer Debt

Annual Income $50,000, Annual Expenditure $80,000. Result—Misery

The financial crisis in 2007 was triggered initially by a drop in US house prices. But the biggest problem was not the housing market. It was debt. After more than a quarter of a century of steadily rising consumption and stagnant real incomes, the savings of many American and European families had collapsed while borrowing had spun out of control.

For decades, until the mid-1980s, the average American family saved between 8 percent and 12 percent of what it earned. Americans saved for that rainy day their grandparents had warned them about, for any medical treatment they might one day need, and for their retirement.

But as the economy continued to grow during the 1990s many people began to think less about saving and more about spending. Unemployment was low and people were being encouraged by policy makers to consume, not save. The temptation to spend was made even easier because money had become so simple to borrow. If people needed money for an operation, a new car, or a bigger house they could get it from a bank. Saving was yesterday's story.

At the time, America's banks were awash with money and were desperate to lend. Thanks partly to the integration of Asian economies into the global banking system, many Western banks had more money than they knew what to do with.

This made it easy for Americans to get a mortgage. As a result, the demand for housing began to rise, causing house prices, in turn, to increase. This made the market even more attractive for the banks and so they gradually became less fussy about whom they lent to. They made fewer checks to see if borrowers were able to pay back the loans. At the same time, American families began to save less, until by 2006 they put aside just 1 percent of what they earned. Many had no savings at all.

The fashion for lending and spending quickly got out of control. As the banks lent more, house prices rose even faster. So, as they were unrestrained by the regulators, the banks lent yet more. Offering loans for cars or raising credit card limits was only a small step further and offered even better returns. The economy was growing, jobs were plentiful and many of those wanting to borrow already owned houses that were rising in value. If the credit or store-card loan went sour, the bank could always force the borrower to sell his home. Few people thought about natural economic cycles, or considered the fact that house prices could also fall.

An important twist in the story was the role of "securitization," a complex term for something that is actually quite simple. Securitization is the word used when banks package together a group of loans, such as mortgages, and sell them to investors as "securities," negotiable instruments that can be bought and sold.

Securitization made it possible for banks to raise more money by selling the mortgages they had made. This allowed them to offer even more mortgages. Then they could securitize these too, and have yet more money to lend.

There were many buyers for these securitized mortgage loan packages. Pension funds and insurance companies around the world were sodden with baby-boomer cash too, looking for somewhere to invest it. Getting a slice of the rising US housing market was just the ticket.

To be sure they were investing safely, pension funds and insurance companies relied on credit ratings agencies. These independent companies, such as Moody's or Standard & Poor's, were responsible for giving the securitized mortgage packages a "rating." If the home loans in a package had been made to wealthy people with good payment records, the rating agency might give the package of mortgages a coveted triple-A or "prime" rating—the top level. As far as buyers of these securitized loans were concerned, they were as safe as government bonds.

As time went on, however, the banks started lending more recklessly. They began lending to people without credit histories, without fixed incomes. But it was hard for them to guarantee the quality of mortgages offered to people like this, people without jobs. These were not triple-A customers, they were "sub-prime." Who would want to buy a load of suspect loans made to individuals with a high risk of default?

To get around this problem, the banks began to repackage their loans, mixing many safe ones with some very unsafe ones. With house prices still rising, the rate of defaults on even the riskiest loans was still low, so it was easy to pass off these sub-prime loans as safe. This allowed the banks to persuade the ratings agencies, who the banks paid to provide the ratings, to give these mixed-loan packages a better score.

Gradually, a tidal wave of money flowed through the global financial system, pushing up house prices in the US, Spain, Britain, Ireland and many other parts of the world to dizzying heights. Prices rose not because houses were worth more but because people could borrow more and so pay more.

While the regulators dozed, intoxicated by the belief that markets run themselves, loans were made to ever-riskier borrowers, repackaged with even more questionable logic and then re-sold. Then, as happens in all bubbles, the market suddenly collapsed. US house prices stopped growing. Almost overnight borrowers, banks and investors found themselves sitting on a huge, risky pile of debt they could not repay.

When the crisis hit, many Western banks had lent far more than their balance sheets could stand. Having bought or guaranteed so many of these dubious securitized mortgage packages, pension funds and insurance companies were also overloaded with questionable investments. Many financial institutions did not have enough capital to cover their losses and so governments had to bail them out. Although some quickly went bankrupt, others, including some of the biggest in the world such as Citibank, Bank of America, AIG and The Royal Bank of Scotland, were effectively nationalized.

For consumers, who had taken out mortgages on homes they could not afford there was no such bail out. Many filed for bankruptcy or sent the keys to their homes back to the banks. But most struggled on, their plight made worse by their lack of savings. Instead of being prepared for the rainy day their grandparents told them about, millions of people suddenly realized they were sitting on a great deal of debt with empty piggy banks.

Most of this debt remains and it has global consequences. Banks will have to be thrifty for years to put their balance sheets back in order. To pay back what they have borrowed, millions of American and European consumers will need to save more and spend less. As Western citizens cut back, factories across the world will need to reduce their output.

Of course, many hope that this decline in spending in the West will be compensated for by fast-growing developing economies such as those of China or India. The world economy, so driven by consumption, goes the thinking, will be saved if the Chinese and Indians start spending more. But consumer spending in China is less than 20 percent of the level in America, and the Chinese like to save. For every \$10 a US consumer spent in 2010, a Chinese consumer spent \$0.42. Indians spent just a third of that. With consumption in China and India worth only 6 percent of global gross domestic product (GDP), it will take a very long time indeed before the spending of consumers in these countries can make up the shortfall.

The Long Haul for Consumers

This process of "de-leveraging," of consumers paying back their debts and replacing their savings, will be prolonged. The debts are too large for them to be repaid quickly.

At the end of 2009 total US consumer debt, including mortgages, stood at \$13.5 trillion—\$130,000 per household or \$45,000 per head. The average American family owed 2.9 times what it earned. To pay this off in a managed way, even without a rise in interest rates, will take between twenty and thirty years.

Of course, this is only looks at one side of the financial equation. It is just the debt. It ignores the assets of America's consumers. The assets of US households at the end of 2009 stood at $55 trillion according to the Federal Reserve, four times the level of debt.

So where is the problem?

The trouble is, the debts and assets are not evenly spread. The richest thirty million Americans own 70 percent of the assets, worth about $39 trillion. At the other end of the financial spectrum, 120 million Americans had an average net wealth of just $920. More than 24 percent[1] of households—twenty-five million American homes—had *no* marketable assets at all in 2010.

This imbalance between assets and debts explains why more than two million American homes were repossessed in 2009 and why a further 7.4 million[2] were in delinquency or the early stages of foreclosure. Another million were already bank-owned. In the first half of 2010, 24 percent of American homes were worth less than the mortgage[3] taken to buy them. Sub-prime loan delinquencies were running at more than 35 percent; retail credit card delinquencies at 13 percent; and other credit card defaults at more than 11 percent. And all this was at a time when interest rates were almost zero. With house prices still falling, people and businesses were filing for bankruptcy at the rate of 150,000 a month in 2010—1.8 million a year.

In the UK the situation was even worse. Total UK personal debt, including mortgages, stood at $2.2 trillion in 2010—161 percent of household income, higher than America. Personal debts were also out of control in Canada (140 percent debt-to-income ratio, 2009), many other parts of Europe (Netherlands, 241 percent; Spain, 125 percent; Denmark, 272 percent; Ireland, 199 percent—all 2009[4]), as well as in Australia (155 percent, 2009) and South Korea (153 percent, 2008). In all of these countries the ratio of debt to income had grown hugely between 2000 and 2008, typically by 30 to 40 percent.

This debt mountain has to be reduced and the only way this is possible is if consumer spending in all of these countries falls for a prolonged time. That means global economic activity has to fall too.

Bank Debt

> I sincerely believe . . . that banking establishments are more dangerous than standing armies.
>
> THOMAS JEFFERSON, 1816

Unfortunately, it is not just consumers who have been badly overstretched by the spending and lending binge in the developed world during the last thirty years. The debts of the man on the street are trifles compared to those facing many banks, pension funds and insurance companies.

In the nineteenth century, the financial services sector accounted for just 1.5 percent of US economic activity. But by the peak of the stock market bubble in 1929 it had risen dramatically to 6 percent. After the Great Crash this share fell back to 2 percent. So banks have a history of growing wildly during bubbles, partly because they cause them, and then fading again afterwards.

Since the beginning of the 1980s, when the finance sector was deregulated under Reagan, its share of developed-world economic activity has risen steadily, with the fastest growth between 2002 and 2009. In 2009, the financial services industry accounted for 8.4 percent of American GDP,[5] the highest level ever. The story was the same in Britain and many other developed countries where restrictions on the financial sector were eased. Britain's financial services business was worth 8.3 percent of GDP in 2009; it employed almost half a million people and brought in more than $100 billion in tax revenues, 12 percent of the total.

Banks grew partly as a result of a more liberal legislative environment, which allowed them to offer new products, but also because they were now able to leverage their own assets. They borrowed, securitized and traded in options, futures and derivatives in many multiples of their capital base. This allowed them to make much higher profits—but also to take much greater risks.

Banks also grew in less transparent ways, which were difficult for regulators to follow. They developed ever more complex financial products that even many central bankers found hard to understand. They opened off-shore financial centers to evade domestic laws. And they adopted weird accounting policies that gave a misleading picture of their financial health. These included the use of complex trades known as "repos" that allowed liabilities to be shown as assets. Lehman Brothers hid $50 billion of liabilities this way before it went bust.

They were allowed to do this despite the fact regulators knew the risks inherent in the finance sector were grave. Banks have ruined the lives of many people over the centuries, not just in the aftermath of the Great Crash. Bankers have a well-deserved reputation for being greedy and for lending too much when times are good. They conveniently forget the previous crashes and crises they have caused. Without control, they can even create asset bubbles deliberately, just to make money.

Big banks are said to carry "moral hazard." This means that because they are large and important to the financial system, and because so many people depend on them, they can take risks without worrying about the consequences. They know that governments will have to bail them out if things go wrong. If there are too many big banks that become too closely interlinked or dependent on the same sources of revenue, they are said to carry "systemic" risk. If they get into trouble together there is a risk that the whole economic system will collapse with them.

This is why banks need to be tightly regulated.

Despite these risks, the activities of the financial sector were greatly ignored by regulators during the boom years. The invisible hand was king. Alan Greenspan, who was the head of the Federal Reserve in America during most of this time, was probably the most important man who had his hand off the regulatory rudder. For years he was held as a hero, a magician who could maintain steady growth with a light touch and little intervention. Despite knowing the risks, he believed what the economists had told him—that the invisible hand would address any problems.

He worshipped at the altar of self-correcting markets. He even claimed to be in a state of "shocked disbelief" when the bubble burst. He said it was hard to predict radical shifts in markets, but this is difficult to believe. His undergraduate thesis was on economic discontinuities that come from house-price bubbles.

Greenspan's misplaced belief in the power of the market, along with that of many other central bankers, led to a crisis that previous generations could easily have foreseen. The free-market philosophy allowed the banking sector to become too large and grow too quickly, making it impossible to manage or understand. Faulty economic ideas allowed many of the West's biggest banks to take massive risks, which were not in society's interests.

Since 2007, the consequences of this wrong-headedness have become easier to see. The IMF estimates that US losses from the banking sector will eventually reach $1.1 trillion, with banks having to write off more than 8 percent of their loans. This looks optimistic. With a quarter of US home owners struggling to pay their mortgages in 2010, and more than a third of credit card holders delinquent, final write-offs could easily be twice that.

In the UK, banks accumulated liabilities of $11 trillion,[6] in an economy less than a fifth of the size of the US's. At one point the Bank of Scotland had housing loans outstanding of more than $400 billion and a capital base of just $15 billion. The Royal Bank of Scotland (RBS), which had to be taken under state control when its stock market value fell by 96 percent to just $5 billion, had become one of the biggest banks in the world, with outstanding loans of almost $3 trillion—one and a half times British GDP. The IMF[7] estimates that UK banks will need to write off 7 percent of their loans—equal to almost 35 percent of Britain's GDP. Similar liabilities exist in Iceland, Ireland, Greece, Spain, Portugal and many other European countries.

So, it is not just consumer spending that will be cut in the years ahead. Bank lending is going to be restricted for years too, as many of the world's biggest banks put their balance sheets in order.

The Sorry Story of Freddie and Fannie

In the US there are also the liabilities of America's Federal National Mortgage Association (Fannie Mae) and Federal Home Loan

Mortgage Corporation (Freddie Mac) to consider. These are not included in the IMF's calculations or in the government's accounts.

Fannie Mae and Freddie Mac were originally government-backed institutions that bought mortgages from banks and other lenders. They securitized these to provide liquidity for the housing market.

During the financial crisis it transpired that Fannie and Freddie had more liabilities than all the other US financial institutions combined. They held, or guaranteed, mortgage-backed securities worth $5.5 trillion; the largest non-governmental debt pile in the world. They also held many of the worst loans, those with the smallest levels of owner-equity, and a large share of loans in states where house prices were falling fastest. Both were taken under government "conservatorship" in 2008 to prevent them from going bankrupt. To do so, the federal government had to raise the ceiling for national debt to $10.5 trillion.[8] It was the biggest bailout in American history.

By mid-2010, Fannie and Freddie had already been refinanced to the extent of $160 billion. Estimates of their eventual total losses vary. Many believe the losses will rise to $1 trillion,[9] $3,000 for every American citizen.

The problems facing Fannie and Freddie have widespread implications. Banks, pension funds, sovereign wealth funds and small savers hold billions of dollars of their debt. According to the Federal Reserve, foreign governments, including those of China and Japan, held Fannie and Freddie bonds with a face value of $908 billion in 2010. By any reasonable measure, this investment is completely worthless.

The A-Bomb Is Ticking

If it were not bad enough that so many of the world's financial institutions are laden with debts big enough to cripple many of the developed world's economies for years, there are pot-holes in the road ahead that will make things worse.

One of these is adjustable-rate mortgages. These are also known as Alt-A, balloon, Option ARM (optional-payment adjustable-rate mortgage) and reset mortgages. It is not for fun that these are called "nightmare loans."

Many people took out these loans during the boom times, when house prices were rising fastest, during 2003 to 2007.

Typically, they offered low rates of interest and very low monthly payments. But they often contained a clause, which meant that after four or five years the rate of interest would be "reset." This could mean that the monthly payments increased dramatically. Or it could mean that the entire loan would be due for repayment.

They were loans that appeared deceptively simple but they contained hidden traps for the financially naive. In a rising market they were shoddy financial products. In a falling one they were a potential disaster for borrowers and lenders alike.

Many people taking out these loans did not understand what they were buying. They were "financial innocents," unused to dealing with silver-tongued finance brokers or managing so much debt. The small print in the contracts was also extremely complex. Few borrowers understood that because the monthly payments were so low the total debt actually increased each month despite their regular payments.

Salesmen were paid extra to sell these loans. To push them through quickly and make a commission, the borrower's ability to pay was often ignored. It did not matter if the borrowers were making a foolish decision that could push them towards insolvency. Selling the loans came first. Stories of unemployed tomato farmers in New Mexico buying homes for nearly one million dollars without any down payment abound.

Many people took on loans, which, at normal rates of interest, they could never afford. They hoped, and were encouraged to believe that, over time, they could make a profit on the house they were buying. When the mortgage was reset they could sell the house, take the gain, and move on.

But because house prices fell, many of these borrowers did not experience any gain. They will not be able to afford the hefty monthly payments when the rates are reset in the years ahead. They have loans they cannot afford, which are bigger than when they started, and houses that are worth a fraction of the debt.

More than $750 billion of these mortgages were sold between 2004 and 2007 and most have yet to roll-over; many of them are due to reset in 2011 and 2012. With economic activity still likely to be weak, these will bring another round of mortgage defaults and further house price declines as owners are forced to sell. Personal bankruptcies will rise further.

America's middle classes, not the poor, were the biggest buyers of these nightmare loans. Many will have to walk away from their homes, leaving the banks to carry yet more losses.

Most of these loans were made by Golden West, now part of Wells Fargo; Bank of America; and JPMorgan Chase. But losses on variable rate loans will also affect hedge and other investment funds. No one knows what this will mean—again because of a failure by regulators to monitor what was going on. Banks did not have to report how many of these types of loans they had underwritten. George McCarthy, a housing economist at New York's Ford Foundation, likens the coming problem to an atom bomb. "It's going to kill all the people but leave the houses standing," he says.

Europe's $40 Trillion Headache

In Europe there is a different problem. Most European banks have not securitized their loans. They appear on the banks' balance sheets. Instead, they are financed through borrowing that has been refinanced periodically. This means that they have massive refinancing needs in the coming years. According to Standard & Poor's, the total liabilities of European banks were equal to more than two-thirds of global GDP in 2010—$30 trillion for the eurozone and $10 trillion for the UK, Sweden, and Denmark.

Banks will have to roll over these loans in a crowded market, competing with debt-hungry states. By 2012, about 1 trillion of such debt in the eurozone and Britain will become due. This is likely to push up interest rates. Banks in countries where loans are most at risk, such as Greece, Ireland and Spain, may face particular problems.

You Still Expect a Pension?

A further worry concerns the insurance, investment fund and pensions sectors, as these hold much of the developed world's savings. They, too, have invested vast amounts rather foolishly, in housing and in the bubble economy that the developed world created. They, too, rode the wave.

Across the developed world, pension funds are burdened with shortfalls they will now struggle to make up. In 2008, the US corporate pensions' shortfall was between 25 percent and 30 percent of the amount needed to meet retirement obligations. In many other countries the shortfall is even higher.

Because of the gap between payments that are due to be made and the amount available to pay them, many pension funds, life assurance providers and investment specialists will be unable to deliver on their promises. Many pensioners in the West will receive less than they expected forcing them to cut spending even more in the years ahead. It will also affect house prices as the elderly sell homes to live off the proceeds.

People will have to work longer too, although this is not as unreasonable as it might first appear. When most retirement funds were set up in the West people worked until they were sixty or sixty-five years old. They could expect to enjoy five or ten years of retirement before they died. Today, many people in Europe expect to retire in their fifties or early sixties. They also live far longer. A working life of forty-five years spent saving for a retirement of five or ten years made sense. A working life of thirty or thirty-five years with a retirement of another thirty or thirty-five years does not. It is little wonder that some US states are raising the compulsory retirement age to eighty-five or ninety years old.

The insurance sector is another business that is vulnerable. Many Western insurers have underwritten the financial risks in their economies. They provided policies for home owners and banks, protecting them from mortgage default and losses. American insurance exposure to the US housing sector was valued at $460 billion in 2009, much of this covering loans made by Fannie and Freddie.

Of course many global financial institutions remain strong despite this catalogue of catastrophe in the West. Most banks in Asia, the Middle East and Africa are reasonably secure. Even here, though, there are concerns, especially concerning banks in China. Between 1998 and 2007 Chinese banks received $434 billion in government bailouts, a huge sum in a country of its economic size. In 2008, the Agricultural Bank of China alone wrote off bad loans worth $120 billion.[10] China also has one of the fastest aging populations in the world. As the elderly retire there will be a drain on savings and a change in consumer spending patterns here too.

Government Debt

The third part of the tale of financial troubles caused by an over-enthusiasm for free-market economics concerns many of the world's biggest governments. If the numbers before were horrible, these ones get even scarier.

To Understand Japan Is To Avoid It: Perhaps

The bleakest financial outlook is in Japan, the world's third biggest economy. Although other countries are not in such serious trouble several, such as Italy, Greece, Ireland and the UK, are heading that way. If they continue to borrow many more, including the US, will face Japan's fate too.

Japan has had more than twenty years of recession since an economic bubble there burst in 1989. Yet a visitor, at least to Tokyo, could be forgiven for thinking that nothing much was wrong. The streets are pristine, crime is low and there remains a sense of decency and pride in people's faces. A trip to the countryside reveals a different picture. More people sleep on the streets, businesses are closed up and there is a sense of rising poverty with the growth in low-cost food stores. You can feel how far the country has slipped and how long it has taken to get there. Japan's citizens have been on a slow-moving conveyor belt for twenty years, which has been taking them ever further downwards. All they can see ahead is more of the same.

Japan is burdened by deflation, massive public debt, an aging population and political stagnation. The economy is shrinking. Japan's GDP in 2009 was lower *in nominal terms* than in 1991. But the debts are still growing. The government's 2010 budget required borrowings of $468 billion, while tax revenues only amounted to $390 billion. This is like earning $39,000 a year but having outgoings of $86,000. To make matters worse, Japan already had huge debts. Its debt-to-GDP ratio is more than 200 percent, equal to seventeen years of tax payments.

It is impossible to pay this off. Japan has debts of $10 trillion, and the amount it borrows is rising by almost $500 billion a year, while tax revenues bring in barely enough to pay the interest. The numbers don't add up. It is only because the Japanese government has been able to borrow at low rates of interest from the bank accounts of frugal Japanese savers that the country has been able to survive economically at all. When these savings are exhausted, Japan will either have to pay international rates of interest or stop borrowing. If the country keeps borrowing, it will go bankrupt. If it stops borrowing, with such a tiny tax take compared to the level of outgoings, the economy will hit a wall.

Japan is No Longer Alone

America's level of government debt is not as bad as Japan's. But America's federal debts have been rising fast and are getting too large. They doubled between 2003 and 2010 to reach $14 trillion—equivalent to 94 percent of US GDP, a peace-time record. To pay them off would need almost three times the amount of gold ever mined in the history of humanity at 2010 prices.

The US government had an income from taxes and fees of $2.2 trillion in 2010,[11] 16 percent less than in 2007. It had expenditure of $3.7 trillion. This meant that in just one year the deficit increased by a further $1.55 trillion—or a further $4,700 for every US citizen. It was like borrowing the entire amount needed for the pensions and healthcare budgets that year.

Because interest rates were very low, the cost of servicing this debt in 2010 was only $187 billion. At more typical rates of interest, say 2 percent, it would have cost an additional $100 billion more. At that rate, just paying off the interest each year would require the government to spend 13 percent of its budget—more than one in every eight US tax dollars paid. Much of this interest would be paid abroad because most of the debt is financed by other countries. For every $100 each American paid in taxes in 2010, $8.50 was used to pay the interest on America's debts. Of this, $4 was paid to China, Japan, the UK and others.

Nor was the $14 trillion debt mountain stated in the US government's accounts in 2010 the whole picture. It did not include the government's liabilities for Fannie and Freddie, which were deemed "off balance sheet." Assuming these reach $1 trillion, they add another seven percentage points to America's federal debts, taking the ratio to 108 percent of GDP in 2011. Nor do the government's figures include federal guarantees for mutual funds, banks, and corporations. These covered risks of a further $19.9 trillion[12] at the end of 2009.

To get the full picture, we also need to include state and local government borrowing. Added together, gross US public debt in 2010 was $16.6 trillion, or $50,000 per US citizen.

There is, as yet, no serious plan to cut this. By 2020, the government's debts will exceed $22 trillion, four times the level in 2000. According to the Congressional Budget Office, almost half the increase between 2009 and 2019 will be the result of interest costs alone. In 2020, interest payments will exceed $910 billion, or more than 40 percent of total federal tax revenues in 2010.

Even this is not the full picture. It ignores what are known as the unfunded future liabilities.

The US government has legal obligations to make health and social security payments in the future, mostly to federal, state and local government employees—teachers, policemen, prison guards and other government workers. These currently exceed projected tax revenues by a further $48 trillion. They are "known" commitments that need to be paid out in addition to normal spending. Yet they are "unfunded," in that there are no funds put aside to pay them. To meet these obligations will either require additional taxes or yet more borrowing. The total value of unfunded liabilities amounted to $412,400 per US household in 2010. By 2013 they will reach $474,077.[13]

Thankfully, these unfunded commitments are not all due immediately. The Medicare commitments, which amounted to $36 trillion in 2010, span the next seventy-five years.

But they still mean that the choice facing America is a stark one. Either these obligations need to be reduced—by cutting pensions

Table 3.1 American financial liabilities per head in 2010

	US dollars
Average personal debt	45,000
Share of gross public debt	50,000
Unfunded Medicare and social security	145,000
Additional Fannie and Freddie liabilities	>3,000
Other bank debt which needs to be written off[14]	>3,500
Federal guarantees to mutual funds, banks, and corporations	unknown*
Total	>246,500

**If the federal guarantees provided have to be written off with the same ratio as other bank debt at 8.3 percent of the $19.9 trillion guaranteed, this would add a further $5,005 per person.*

or reneging on medical insurance promises—or they will have to be funded by future generations. That will be tough. Future generations will also have to pay off much of the other debt and to do this they will have to pay higher taxes. Asking them to pay the pensions and rising medical costs of retirees means they will need to be taxed at untenable levels.

Adding these debts together does not make a pretty picture. In 2010, every US citizen had average liabilities of at least $245,000 (see Table 3.1). This is more than $80 trillion, six times US GDP. It would take thirty-seven years of 2010 tax revenues to pay these debts off, more than twice as long as in Japan. For each US household, the debt in 2010 was more than $735,000.

This government debt "mountain" is not just in the US and Japan. Government debt is also high and rising in Italy, Greece, Germany, France, Israel, Canada and Spain. Britain's debt-to-GDP ratio will almost double between 2007 and 2012 and continue to rise thereafter. In 2010 the UK incurred interest costs of $127 million a day—adding a further burden of $1,890 per household. The total pensions' shortfall in the UK stood at $6 trillion[15] in 2010 and is still growing. At almost three times the country's GDP, this alone will require an "intergenerational transfer" of funds according to Britain's Office for National Statistics. If today's British citizens want to remove this burden from their children they would need to pay 30 percent more tax each year. They are unlikely to want to do that. Instead, they will leave each, as-yet-unborn, person with a $300,000 tax bill.

Throughout most of the developed world there is a government debt burden which is increasingly unmanageable. Worse, it is still growing. No matter where you live on the planet this mountain of debt will affect you. If the wealthiest 60 percent of the world economy is forced to change the way it spends, the other 40 percent will not remain unscathed.

Who Is to Blame for All This, Other than the Economists?

The global financial mess we are in is not only the fault of free-market-obsessed economists. They simply justified a system that others then used. The politicians are also to blame. To secure re-election, they wanted to believe that they could manufacture endless economic growth. The industrialists also carry responsibility. They wanted everyone to spend, to keep their factories operating and the dividends flowing. The bankers are guilty too. They wanted to make money without giving any thought about the effects on society. And Western consumers have also behaved badly. They wanted to spend without any consequences.

There are other culprits, many of them. The legislators, mainly the central bankers, clearly played a role in this failure, accepting so enthusiastically the free-market siren call. American central bankers saw far ahead that trouble was brewing in the domestic and commercial real-estate sectors. They knew that bank lending was getting out of hand. "Frothy" was the word used by Alan Greenspan to describe the situation when he was chairman of the Federal Reserve. This was hopelessly irresponsible: it made an unstable economic situation seem as harmless as a warming pan of milk. It led him and others to take a sanguine perspective, to believe that all was well, to believe that the free market and the rational behavior of consumers would eventually fix the problem.

Given the scale of the debt and the millions who will be affected in future generations, there should be a case for Alan Greenspan and Hank Paulson to be charged with economic crimes against humanity. The suffering they will bring, in terms of misery, ill health and poverty, is a disgrace.

The Federal Reserve and many other central banks listened to the self-serving pleas of greedy bankers, failed to see that asset prices were being pushed up because credit was too freely available, and then claimed to be in shock, at least at first, when the bubble burst. They then compounded their mistakes by encouraging governments to borrow heavily and print money.

Although there is evidence that some central bankers felt they were under political pressure during the boom years, this does not excuse them. Central bankers are meant to be independent and strong. Property bubbles and irresponsible lending can, and should, be controlled—they can even be eradicated. In some parts of Europe property bubbles do not happen. Speculations in housing and unfair gains are curtailed through taxation. Leaving bubbles for the market to fix is not just unnecessary, it was also, in this case, a dreadful mistake. The irresponsibility or incompetence of a few will lead to long-term suffering for millions. That was not what Smith had in mind when he talked about the invisible hand.

Regulators of questionable competence, with too much faith in the theories of modern economics, also allowed banks to become pillars of the free-market system. They sat and watched while many of them took advantage of their position, flooding economies with debt, allowing a minority of people to become excessively rich. Through inaction, banks were able to take risks large enough to undermine the West's economic foundations.

Despite the consequences of these errors, regulators have still done almost nothing to curb banks' activities. Even today, the world's big banks remain a massive source of financial instability, untamed and unrepentant.

That will have to change.

Similarly, the credit ratings agencies should be held accountable. They failed to rate debts properly, providing those who saved and regulators with a dangerously misleading picture. They allowed themselves to get into a business where they had clear conflicts of interest.

Most damning of all, these agencies are still getting it wrong today. Despite having unsustainable debts, the bonds issued by the governments of the US and UK still had triple-A ratings from the top three credit ratings companies (Fitch, Standard & Poor's and Moody's) in 2010. Tellingly, China's ratings agency, Dagong, took a different view and has stripped the US, UK, Germany and France of their triple-A status.

We will look at the implications of these financial problems in chapter nine and at the options we face in the last three chapters.

Endnotes

1. Edward N. Wolff, "Recent Trends in Household Wealth in the United States: Rising Debt and the Middle-Class Squeeze—an Update to 2007," Levy Economics Institute of Bard College, Working Paper No. 589, March 2010. http://www.levyinstitute.org/publications/?docid=1235.
2. "Lender Processing Services' December 2009 Mortgage Monitor Report Reveals One in Every 7.5 Properties Behind on Payments or in Foreclosure," January 2010. http://www.lpsvcs.com/LPSCorporateInformation/NewsRoom/Pages/20100120.aspx.
3. First American Core Logic, "January Home Price Index Shows Narrowing Annual Decline According to Newly Released First American CoreLogic Date," March 18, 2010. http//www.facorelogic.com/newsroom/pressreleasedetails.jsp?id=10668.
4. Eurostat, Gross debt-to-income ratio of households is defined as loans (ESA95 code: AF4).
5. Bureau of Economic Analysis "Gross Output by Industry" report, 1998–2009. http://www.bea.gov/industry/gdpbyind_data.htm.
6. See "Assessing State Support in the UK Banking Sector," Oxera Report, March 11 2011, Executive Summary page two, converted into USD. http://www.oxera.com/cmsDocuments/Assessing%20state%20support%20to%20the%20UK%20banking%20sector.pdf. Also Office of National Statistics Report, January 2009.
7. IMF Global Stability Report. http://www.ft.com/intl/cms/s/0/bc2b14b0-2eb8-11de-b7d3-00144feabdc0.html.
8. The Federal Reserve also bought a further $1.4 trillion of bad loans from Fannie and Freddie.
9. Lorraine Woellert and John Gittelsohn, "Fannie-Freddie Fix at $160 Billion With $1 Trillion Worst Case," Bloomberg, June 14, 2010. http://www.bloomberg.com/apps/news?pid=20601109&sid=an_hcY9YaJas&pos=10.

10. *The Economist*, "Listing or capsizing? A huge public offering tests global sentiment about China," June 10, 2010. http://www.economist.com/node/16319645.

11. U.S. Government Revenue, "Total Budgeted Government Revenue," 2010. http;//www.usgovernmentrevenue.com/#usgs302a.

12. "US Taxpayer Exposure Financial Bailouts of 2008." http://www.usfederalbailout.com/program_details.

13. *A Roadmap For America's Future*, "A Plan To Solve America's Long-Term Economic And Fiscal Crisis" Representative Paul D. Ryan, Committee on the Budget, May 2008.

14. IMF estimated figure that 8.3 percent of outstanding bank debt will be written off.

15. Sean O' Grady, "Britain's debt: The untold story," The Independent (UK), July 14, 2010. http://www.independent.co.uk/news/uk/politics/britainrsquos-debt-the-untold-story-2025979.html.

4

SQUANDERING OUR WORLD

Nature, to be commanded, must be obeyed.

Sir Francis Bacon

Who Owns the World's Resources?

The financial consequences of modern economic thinking are bad, but they are less serious than the environmental ones.

You don't have to work for Greenpeace to see that what we are doing to our planet is not sustainable. We are heating it up with potentially catastrophic consequences. We are polluting the rivers and skies. We are emptying the oceans of fish and the forests of trees and animals. We will leave our grandchildren a wasteland unless we stop.

In 1968 R. Buckminster Fuller wrote *Operating Manual for Spaceship Earth*. He saw us as astronauts flying through space on a ship with a fixed amount of resources. When we have used them up, they are gone.

Although it was not written as an assault on modern economics, parts of it could have been. Fuller talked about the problems of the world's resources being taken over by "the Great Pirates," a small group of greedy people. They were able to do this because everyone else was unaware of what they were really up to. The pirates manipulated information, opened trade routes and then controlled the world's raw materials for their own benefit.

Central to the way we look at the world's resources today is a question most of us have forgotten to ask: To whom do the world's resources belong? Do they belong to the world? Do they belong to humankind? Do they belong to all species? Do they belong to whoever controls them?

Once we answer that question, we will know how we should price, allocate and use the world's resources.

During the last thirty years, following the *laissez-faire* ideas of the new economists, we have increasingly believed that the best way to allocate the world's resources is through the free market. In so doing, however, we have made a grave error. The notion of the free market we use today has badly mis-priced them. It has encouraged their misuse.

Moreover, many of us appear to have adopted the views of China's Chairman Mao, which are the opposite of Sir Francis Bacon's enlightenment views. While Bacon believed that we are answerable to nature, Mao believed that nature should be bent to the will of humankind. Mao's thinking encourages us to abuse nature for profit and to ruin ecosystems without considering their full value to us or to future generations. It makes us believe their depletion does not matter.

The world's natural resources are either finite, as with water, or become depleted as they are used and transformed into something else, as with coal or oil.

There is a fixed amount of water on the planet, a tiny fraction of which is drinkable. Although we use it, it is recycled through the hydro-cycle, and so we get it back again. The main concern for resources like water is the rise in population and the pollution of the water we have. In the past we had more than enough water to go around, but with seven billion people there is not enough available now for every person.

For fossil fuels like oil and gas, and most other natural resources, it is different. As they are used, the amount remaining declines. Although, technically, all the chemical elements remain after we use them, they cannot be reconstituted. We can use them only once. This also means that their price goes up as they get consumed. There is less remaining and it becomes more difficult to find and extract what is left.

As we saw in the last chapter, consumption is the fuel for our modern economic engine, but to consume more means we must use more of the world's resources. Common sense—and classical economics—says that we should use them carefully, not just because they are precious but also because many are finite. We have a duty to society, to other peoples, and to future generations.

Despite this, modern economics actually encourages us to waste them.

To boost consumption, we now sell more and more products that are disposable. We also design products that have a much shorter life than necessary, and items that are increasingly subject to fads and fashions. We do this partly for our convenience, but also because it allows us to generate higher levels of consumption and so more growth, which is our main measure of progress. It is perfectly possible to design and build a car or washing machine that lasts thirty years. But we choose, instead, to make them last eight or so years, to boost sales, employment and growth.

Modern economics has changed the way we look at resources, encouraging us to use them faster and to waste much of what is left. Classical economics theories advocated the use of the "market" to allocate resources too. But Smith's theories were underpinned by a strong belief in a sense of fairness and a desire to achieve the optimal outcome for society.

To be "efficient," markets needed to have rules.

One rule is that they must have a great deal of competition. Smith believed that monopoly power was damaging, whether it stemmed from unions or a handful of companies dominating a market. So, to him, the idea that a small group of companies should control access to many of the world's natural resources, as they do today, was simply wrong. It leads to exploitation and is to the detriment of society.

Another rule is that producers must always reflect the full costs in their selling price. This is called cost internalization. It says that businesses and individuals need to pay for all the negative external effects of their actions, such as the environmental damage. Classical economic theory says we must pay for the hidden damage we cause. It says that the price we pay for a natural resource today should reflect the loss of that resource to generations in the future. If not, then part of the price of using it today is paid by someone else, our grandchildren. These costs do not go away just because we do not pay them. They are simply being ignored by those who benefit today.

Instead of enforcing even a simple idea, such as the polluter pays, under-regulated markets have encouraged us to reward the cheapest cost-avoider—the company that can provide the cheapest price in the market by avoiding and reducing as many costs as possible. When a logging company clears the rainforest it may pay to use the land; and it will make a profit if it sells the wood. But neither it nor its customers pay for the loss of habitat needed by the animals that lived there, for the loss of environmental diversity, for the destruction of plants we have not yet studied, or for destroying any local culture. By following modern-economics theory we consign those costs to society or to future generations. We do not know if these costs are high or low. So we ignore them and pass them on.

Similarly, when a factory making plastics in China releases its toxic waste into a river, it does not include the cost of its actions in the price it charges the consumer. So the plastic is cheaper than it should be. The people who buy the plastic are being subsidized by those living downstream, who pay part of the cost for it with their ill health. The dead fish and poisoned aquatic life pay part of the cost too, as do the oceans into which the river flows.

In classical economics, the logging company or the plastics manufacturer are said to receive "unearned" profits as a result of their actions. They make a gain that they should not. The theory says that this is inefficient and therefore wrong. Moreover, the consumer of the wood or plastic benefits unfairly too. A lower price is paid than it should be. This gives the consumer an unearned gain and, because the product is cheaper than it should be, an incentive to use more.

You Don't Like These Principles? I Have Others

How have we managed to move from a rational approach, which protects the world, to the irrational model we have today, which does not?

Again, the answer lies in our modern interpretation of economics. We have been re-educated to believe that classical-market economics and today's free-market economics are the same. Rather than forcing us to pay properly, we have been held hostage not just by modern economists but also by corporate libertarians, the post-Reaganites, who tell us that regulation and government interference should be minimized. Regulation would mean higher prices, they say. "How can that be in the interests of hard-working men and women and big business?" shout the populist politicians. Almost no one speaks up for nature or the yet-unborn.

The implications of this way of thinking have changed our world. For years, we have rewarded businesses that offered lower prices and made higher profits. This encouraged companies to externalize as many costs as they could. To attract investors and create jobs, countries fought to offer more favorable conditions. They encouraged low wages, ignored environmental damage, and offered tax incentives and subsidies to international companies. They subsidized humankind's resource use even further, meaning that the end-price of the goods we consumed was cheaper than it should be. This encouraged yet more consumption, waste and over use, fuelling the cycle further.

We'll Know What It's Worth When It's Gone

One of our most under-priced natural resources is oil. For years, we have ignored the environmental costs of extracting and using the stuff, and have barely thought about what using up the world's entire reserves in 150 years will mean for future generations. In many countries the price is subsidized, encouraging even greater waste. According to the International Energy Agency (IEA), the world spent $550 billion subsidizing energy prices in thirty-seven large, developing countries in 2009. Both China and India were among the biggest subsidizers, just as the US was during most of the twentieth century, by using price controls.

Oil is vital to our world and is likely to remain vital to our grandchildren's world too. Most of our land, sea and air transport systems depend entirely on it. We use it to generate electricity. Without it, we would not have many hospital supplies or modern anesthetics.

With such dependence, our failure to price the stuff correctly is likely to prove dangerously short sighted. Like spoilt children, we have not appreciated the value of what we have been given. In doing so, we risk consequences that make the world's finance problems look tame.

Of course, the world's oil is not going to run out any time soon. But what is left is getting harder to extract. Demand is rising too, as developing economies grow. These factors mean that the price will rise steadily in the years to come. Many of the world's biggest oil fields are also in decline, which will push the price up further. According to the US military, surplus capacity could disappear as soon as 2012[1] bringing us shortages of up to 10 million barrels a day by 2015. That is one in every eight barrels used in 2010.

Our economic world has grown in the last thirty years, to a large extent because of wrongly priced oil. Our rapid pace of progress was partly the result of this market failure. As we use up what is left, that failure will correct itself.

As we will see in chapter ten, this correction will change our lives.

Our Rare Earth

It is much the same with many other raw materials. If China and India continue to industrialize rapidly, and try to adopt the same standard of living enjoyed by populations in the US or Europe today, some of the world's most critical resources will be quickly exhausted.

Indium, which is used in liquid crystal displays, is likely to run out within a decade[2] even if our current rate of use remains unchanged. If demand continues to rise, supplies of nickel, antimony and tin will reach a crunch point too. There are also concerns about the remaining reserves of tantalum, used in electronics, aerospace and power generation, and hafnium, used in the nuclear industry. China, which has the largest supply of many rare earths, has now restricted the export of several, including oxides of europium and yttrium. Politicians in India have begun to talk about banning iron ore exports to protect supplies for future generations. Many countries have even banned exports of sand for the construction industry, including Saudi Arabia—the desert kingdom.

As supplies of these and other resources become more depleted, their prices will rise. The grade of many metals remaining will also decline as reserves are exhausted. There will be a tendency for countries and businesses to hoard supplies, knowing they can profit by doing so. Shortages will also encourage theft, as they already have done with copper. When they are gone our industrial development will be constrained.

Just like the trees on Easter Island, which were cut down until there were none left ending the existence of human life on the island, we are using up many of the world's declining resources without much thought for the future. We are not pricing them for the coming generations. Rather than the use of the world's raw materials being controlled by society, they are being exploited for profit. Because of modern-economic thinking, today's businesses are rewarded when they focus on the short term and rising quarterly returns. It is in their interests to outsource the externalities, to ignore the wider societal implications of their actions.

Yet reducing the rate we use resources will be hard. It is difficult to explain to the world's most populous nations that they cannot achieve the same living standards as the West or Japan because the cupboard is now almost bare of some resources. China and India are hardly going to shrug their shoulders when they discover that some of the key resources needed for their development have already been used up, or mostly used up, by Western nations.

One way to manage our resources fairly, for the good of humankind, would be through some sort of supra-national global organization. But this is a wholly unrealistic notion. Even if such a body could be formed, the infighting and desire for control would make it fractious and unstable. But what is the alternative? Continuing to let the free market manage resource allocation perpetuates the under-pricing problem, accelerating the speed with which resources are used. Letting private companies continue to profit from this process will make the imbalances worse. Putting the resources in the hands of national governments is unlikely to work either. It could encourage them to put up trade barriers and increase economic rivalry.

There are no easy answers, although we will look at a few options in the final chapters.

Seven Billion into Water Won't Go

The problem humanity faces with water is different. Like other natural resources water has been undervalued. Unlike the others, though, fixing this anomaly by putting up the price to take proper account of the externalities is probably not a good idea. Given water's importance for our survival, and the inability of many poor people to pay for the stuff, it would be foolish. Instead, the allocation of water needs to be more carefully regulated, set free from the anomalies that have been caused by free-market economics. It is much the same for many foodstuffs.

The other big difference with water is that there are already too many people in the world for the supply of water that we have. There is already a shortage.

The world has a fixed amount of water, most of which lies in the sea. But this is not potable. It can only be used for drinking or irrigation after it has gone through a very energy intensive, expensive and polluting, desalination plant. The bulk of what remains is also not easily usable either, being trapped in glaciers or icecaps. Less than 1 per cent of the water on the planet is potable and readily accessible. Yet this has to be shared among seven billion people as well as all other living things, except those in the sea.

Already, 1.3 billion people do not have access to enough water. They do not have enough to drink or to grow food with. Much of the water they and millions more can access is also polluted, making many people ill. As the population rises in the coming decades, the number of people facing water shortages will increase. By 2050, according to the United Nation's (UN) estimates, more than four people in ten will not have enough water. This is why the UN says that water, or the lack of it, is one of the greatest threats to health, safety, economic growth, human rights and national security that we face.

More than two-thirds of the water we use is needed for food production. So water shortages, if they are not managed, will bring food shortages. In some countries farmers pay for their water but in many they do not. And almost nowhere does the price reflect water's scarcity.

We are making the situation worse by using much of the water we have thoughtlessly, squandering it and polluting many aquifers, rivers and springs. Half the world's wetlands have disappeared in the past 100 years. Lakes are drying up and rivers no longer flow to the sea because we have diverted their water to grow crops. Neither the farmer nor the consumer pays for this. Again, the costs are externalized. While some farmers are allowed to increase the quantities they produce to then sell yet more underpriced cotton and peaches, others downstream are forced into bankruptcy, and city dwellers are forced to ration the water they consume. While some grow fat by planting water-intensive crops in arid lands, ecosystems at river mouths die.

Laissez-Faire, No Thanks

It is especially hard to solve many of these problems using the ideas of modern economics. It is hard to put a price on water, given its importance and uniqueness. Yet there is a vital need to put a value on it somehow, and to manage its use. We also need to find a way to trade it, because some places have plenty of water and others do not. But the free market is unlikely to provide the best answer.

Water, like air, is a unique resource on which we all depend for life. The way we manage water affects the availability of food across the world. There is no moral case for water to be controlled by private companies, which could profit from its use. But thanks to the free marketers, a worrying share of the world's water is already controlled by private companies.

The only obvious solution is for governments to become more involved in managing access to water. If there is to be fairness, regulators will also need to take more control of our food supplies. Partly because of free-market economics and the power of the farming lobby, there is an increasing shortage of land on which to grow food in many countries. This is because we are using some of it to produce bio-fuels, giving greater value to keeping the rich motoring rather than the survival of the poor. Climate change is having a detrimental effect too, and the rate of growth of crop yields is slowing. Other problems include rising energy prices, which in turn affects the cost of fertilizer and the cost of distribution—especially in the developing world where harvests often lie rotting for want of a truck.

According to the UN, the world will need 70 percent more food in the next forty years.

We can achieve this but it will be hard. We will need to use more land in Africa, around the Black Sea and in Latin America. We can also use more genetically modified crops, subject to health fears being properly allayed. But to achieve this target we will need to wean many developing countries off their food subsidies gradually, because these only encourage greater consumption than necessary.

If we use fairness as a principle, many of us will have to reduce the amount of meat in our diets too. Meat production puts great pressure on water supplies and reduces the quantity of grain available for human consumption. Similarly, to meet the world's food requirements we will need to prevent supermarkets and restaurants in developed countries from selling overly cheap food, which has been manufactured or grown by companies outsourcing the externalities of their production. We will need to constrain farmers who use too much water in dry countries. The water industry will also need to do more to contain leaks.

We can also improve the situation by specializing more. We can encourage the production of water-intensive products in wet countries and export these to drier ones. It is wiser to grow beef in rainy Britain than the parched Murray Darling Basin in Australia. We could even introduce punitive taxes on products that use large amounts of water and provide little or no nutritional value, such as carbonated drinks. If every can of cola had a $5 tax, we could reduce water use, lessen obesity, cut healthcare costs and generate revenue simultaneously.

Of course, producing goods in one country and exporting them to another is also dependent on the cost of transportation, which is also under-priced today. Beef shipped from the UK to Australia is likely to be expensive if fuel were correctly priced, which would undermine the possible advantages of specialization. The point is that beef produced in Australia using scarce water resources or exported from Britain needs to be properly priced. If both the supply of water in Australia or the fuel for shipping were priced correctly, the cost of beef for Australian consumers would be much higher than it is today. And so it should be. A higher price would reflect the real costs. It may not be to the liking of Australian meat eaters, but it would be efficient according to the laws of classical economics and better protect the world's resources.

It is difficult to see, however, how such changes can be made using the ideas of modern economics and the free market as many would have us believe. Partly to allay fears of food security, the solutions to the world's food shortages will need prolonged inter-governmental cooperation and trust. Much will depend on how willing we are to adopt enlightenment principles of morality. It is impossible to argue, for example, that it is fair for the poor to pay more for items their lives depend upon, just so someone in the developed world can have a Mercedes. That is not socially responsible.

If the supply of food and water are left under regulated, the world will become even more unequal.

There are many other ways in which our natural world is being abused through improper pricing and the effects of modern-economic thinking. When a boat goes out to sea and comes back with a hold full of fish, in many parts of the world, the fish are apparently free. The boat and the crew cost money, but what they harvest is there for the taking, stolen from the oceans.

Although some attempts have been made to stop this, they have had limited success. To fish in some parts of the world's seas, fishermen now need licenses. Governments have also made a much bigger effort to monitor fish stocks. They have tried to restrict the volumes of fish caught and limit the number of days the trawlers can go out. Yet there are very few cases where these measures have been effective and there are many areas of the seas that are still wholly unregulated. And fishermen often manage to evade the existing regulations. Almost everywhere, fish stocks continue to fall.

Similarly, air pollution levels are still rising around much of the world without any apparent cost. With the growth in population, notably in China and India, more raw sewage and waste is being discharged into our rivers and oceans than ever before, creating dead zones free of oxygen where nothing can survive. We are destroying the world's coral reefs and obliterating the rainforests at the rate of an acre (0.4 hectares) per second. In many cases the timber that is taken costs the loggers nothing. Even where they have to buy a license, these are usually priced to provide the local government with a source of revenue not to protect the environment. As a result, much timber is simply burned along with the animals that lived there.

We are heating up the planet by releasing gases into the atmosphere, which will change weather patterns, food production levels and force us to move away from the areas of many countries that are currently inhabitable. Yet this is done almost without cost.

More worrying, many of these troubles will be made worse by the rise of China, India and many other developing nations. Their economic expansion is increasing the rate at which resources are squandered and the planet is polluted, partly because these nations have little interest in rich-world environmental angst about the long-term consequences. They need progress, growth and consumption as well as food and water—now.

Foreign investors share some of the blame for this too. American, European and other Asian companies have externalized the costs of pollution, energy production and waste by relocating their factories to China and elsewhere. Modern economics has failed to price the costs of this into the end-products we use. Instead, we have let China build coal-fired power plants, kill lakes with poisonous algal blooms and shorten the life expectancy of its citizens. The West has consumed while China and the planet have paid the price.

Modern economics has allowed almost all of us to ignore the costs of our damage to the planet. Yet we all have a responsibility for our world as well as to other species, in whatever form they live. This is partly our moral responsibility as the most intelligent form of life to have evolved. There are also scientific reasons for us to behave more responsibly. We are killing off hundreds of species of plants and animals without understanding the value of their ecosystems. Potential cures for diseases are literally going up in smoke for the sake of a one-time gain, to allow some logger or corrupt official to acquire a Rolex.

We measure progress in terms of growth, which depends on consumption, which needs us to use up more of the world's resources, which is dependent on externalizing costs to cut prices. Yet most of us feel no sense of shame for having allowed this, nor do we accept that we have a responsibility for creating the injustices that have ensued. We need to realize that every bar of soap we buy made from palm oil is adding to the problem.

In 1972, the Club of Rome discussed the sustainability predicament facing humankind. In a report called "*The Limits to Growth,*" the authors said that it was clear that trends in population, food production, industrial production, pollution, and the consumption of non-renewable natural resources would lead to a catastrophe unless our world was better managed. Updates to the report in the last thirty years suggest the original dire predictions still hold true. These forecast the "end of the global system"[3] mid-way through this century.

It does not have to be like this. We can find ways around these problems, or at least many of them. In some cases, we will have to accept that we are up against the laws of chemistry. Much of what we have used and squandered has already been lost for good.

But there is no question that we can achieve a better balance than we have today. Much will depend on the role of government and on better regulation. Economics can play a major role too, as long as it is applied as originally intended.

If we want to act responsibly and think of future generations, however, we cannot continue using the current free-market model to allocate and manage the world's resources. Not only will it not produce the best outcome, it is actually making the situation worse by accelerating the rate of damage and waste.

Endnotes

1. Terry Macalister, "US military warns oil output may dip causing massive shortages by 2015," *The Guardian*, April 11, 2010. http://www.guardian.co.uk/business/2010/apr/11/peak-oil-production-supply.
2. "Dwindling of Rare Metals Imperils Innovation," *InformationWeek*, May 2007.
3. "A comparison of the limits to growth with 30 years of reality," Graham Turner, August 2008.

5

THE DAMAGING POWER OF ME

Earth provides enough to satisfy every man's need,
but not every man's greed.

Mahatma Gandhi

Me, Myself, I

One of the most curious hurdles we need to overcome before we can address humankind's financial and environmental problems is the modern notion of freedom.

That may seem peculiar. Individual freedom lies at the heart of Western thinking and behavior. It is one of the developed world's most treasured concepts: an idea that lies at the core of Western societies. America calls itself "the land of the free" and the former US president, George W. Bush, even said that it was al-Qaeda's hatred of "our freedoms" that made it attack the World Trade Center's Twin Towers in 2001. It is the concept of freedom that America upholds when it goes on so many foreign "adventures."

But what is freedom?

Freedom, as we consider it today, is largely about the individual. It is about the freedom to act as one wishes, without restrictions from authority figures or organizations. According to *Webster's Dictionary*, it is about immunity from obligation. It is about the absence of coercion, the quality of being released. It is about being frank and open. Freedom in America and much of Europe is as much about lifestyle and consumption as it is about social rights. You have the freedom to dress as you wish. You can spend your money as you wish. You can travel as you wish. You can follow the career that you wish. Freedom is a notion warmly wrapped in opportunity and equality.

During the Enlightenment, the concept of freedom was seen differently. Freedom was about thinking, speaking and acting without fear, certainly according to one of its foremost proponents, John Stuart Mill. Mill believed that we must be permitted to consider the world around us without constraints. We must be able to say and do whatever we wish, within reason. He believed that governments should do all they can to remove the barriers to these freedoms, including repealing restrictive laws. He called this "liberty." But he also believed that with freedom comes responsibility. A fundamental principle was that others must not be harmed by an individual acting freely.

The change in the way we think about freedom is important. Mill's concept of freedom carries the same sense of social responsibility that goes with Smith's notion of self interest. Freedom does not mean that mortgage salesmen should sell loans that will lead the borrowers into financial ruin. Freedom does not mean we can rape the planet of its resources. Freedom is not about farmers burning the rainforests and fisherman emptying the seas for short-term gain. None of these actions are in the interests of society. They break the principle of responsibility. The behavior of a few damages the lives of many. The enlightenment concept of freedom involved a vital sense of duty, rather than being about immunity from obligations as it is today.

This change in emphasis affects how we behave—and our motives. Because we are encouraged to be individuals, most of us think about ourselves and our families first. Few of us take much interest in our wider society or in making it better. We rarely consider the social consequences of our actions.

Modern ideas of freedom actually increase inequality and create greater social injustice. Economic wealth does not flow to the brightest, to those who work the hardest, to those who bring the greatest benefit to the greatest number of people, or to the most benevolent. It rewards those individuals and companies that can make the biggest profits by dispersing their costs on to others.

This is in direct conflict with the ideas of Mill, who believed that society has a responsibility to punish and curtail the actions of individuals if they are not in the interests of society. This means that a company should compete fairly with a rival. It should not exploit weak regulations in one country to gain an advantage over rivals in another. That is not in the interests of society.

The Retreat of Conservatism

The rise of neoliberalism and conservatism, particularly in America, risks taking us even further in this direction. Many neoliberals and conservatives strongly believe in the survival of the fittest. They support even more extreme notions of individualism than we have seen in the last thirty years. They believe in minimal government and minimal responsibility to others. This is nature's way, they say. Rather than cooperating, there should be competition between individuals. This leads to winners and losers. It is what evolution is about, they claim. Some conservatives oppose almost any form of government on principle. They are against any restrictions on free markets. To conservatives, survival of the fittest trumps equality and egalitarianism every time.

This is dangerous, certainly from an enlightened perspective. Such thinking leads to a bipolar black-and-white world where informed judgments are unnecessary: it says we should be able to do whatever we want, whenever we want. That is not freedom as Mill understood the idea. Conservatism allows us to think that cooperation is unimportant, that there should been minimal oversight of business and finance, that blind competition for resources and profit are not just the best way, but the only, natural, way. It says that greed need not be restrained. Creative destruction, even when it ends up just being destruction, is part of the process of growth and development. Proponents of neoliberalism and conservatism say there is no point trying to bring the world together to address our challenges, to work towards a common goal, because that is not the way the world works: competition and the market are what work.

Yet this sort of philosophy also eventually breeds instability, because it encourages the rich to get richer, and it makes the lives of the majority gradually more miserable. Eventually, a breaking point comes. As the inequalities grow, the majority will take to the streets or turn to extreme left- or right-wing political parties; to those promising social justice. Ultimately, conservatism leads to some sort of revolution, an upending of the status quo, because it does not provide "fairness." It takes us further in the wrong direction.

Kiasu. Bless You

Modern ideas of freedom and the individual also encourage greed and selfishness, both of which are socially divisive.

In Singapore, there is a word "*kiasu*," which comes from one of the locally-spoken Chinese dialects, Hokkien. Loosely translated it means "must win, never lose." It is a typically Singaporean trait and there is even a local television comedy program based on the idea called *Mr. Kiasu*.

Kiasu means doing almost anything, no matter how inane, to gain at the expense of others. It is driven by the fear of losing and by a desire to frustrate others. When a shop is giving away a free packet of tissues as part of some promotional campaign, a line will form whether those waiting need tissues or not. Many people in Singapore will wait half-an-hour for a free packet of tissues they do not need. When Singaporeans get in an elevator, they will press the door-close button as others approach, just to gain. When driving on Singapore's highways, drivers are advised not to signal before they change lanes. Signaling will only encourage a fellow motorist to move into the spot you need, just to make it awkward for you to overtake or exit. *Kiasu* means filling your plate at a buffet meal with as much of the best and most expensive food as possible, even though you will not eat it—just so no one else can get it.

Kiasu appears trivial and comic and in many ways it is, shockingly so. But it is also the antithesis of enlightened social thinking. It is not about cooperation, or about considering others. It is one of the purest manifestations possible of an individual seeking to gain at the expense of others that there is. It also makes Singapore a singularly unpleasant place to live.

Sadly, it is not just a Singaporean phenomenon. Thanks partly to modern ideas of freedom it exists all over the world, to a greater or lesser extent, even where there is no suitable word for it.

Greed Is Not Good, Gordon

The greed and selfishness that stem from an overly inflated notion of individual freedom have fuelled our mania for consumption. As consumers, we reward low prices without a thought for what this means. As shareholders we reward higher profits, regardless of the social implications. We choose cheaper food, even though it can make us fat and ill, because the cost of our medical treatment will be paid by someone else. We buy items that waste the world's resources because they are cheap.

The Mr. Kiasu within each of us encourages us to support politicians who offer tax cuts, even if they bring misery to millions.

Trying to be humorous, Bush once said that he was in office to support and protect a group he called "the haves and the have mores." He refused to tax the wealthiest, cutting funding on healthcare and student loans instead. His attempt at humor, his actions, and their consequences sent a signal to all of us.

An overly developed sense of individual gain brings unhappiness, because it fuels jealousy, which warps loyalties and principles. It is the thinking behind outsourcing. It encourages huge companies to under invest in their pension plans, or renege on commitments to ex-workers.

Most importantly, the inequalities this thinking causes have been growing.

The typical way inequality is calibrated is by using the Gini coefficient, which measures the distribution of wealth in a society. When the Gini coefficient is zero everyone has an equal share of the available wealth. When it is 100 then one person has all the wealth—that is, there is perfect inequality. One person has all the *kiasu.*

Across the world, the Gini coefficient has been rising steadily—and especially rapidly recently. In the US it was 38 at the end of World War II and it stayed close to that level for the next fifty years. By 2008 however, it had reached 47, a massive jump in a short time.[1] In Brazil, China, the United Kingdom and India too, wealth has become ever more concentrated into the hands of a small group. In 2009 the world had 793 billionaires whose combined net worth was greater than the poorest three billion people.

It has not risen everywhere. It has fallen in countries that have pursued more inclusive social policies, notably Norway and France. While most European countries, as well as Australia and Canada, have coefficients that lie between the mid-20s and the mid-30s, the United States and Mexico stand out. Both have coefficients above 40. In China it now stands at 47, up from 16 in the Mao-era of the 1970s. In *kiasu*-centric Singapore, it was 48 when it was last measured in 2008, higher than almost every other developed country.

This is bad for many reasons. As the Gini coefficient rises, the chances of social unrest occurring grow. It leads to what economists call the "tragedy of the commons." This eventually makes extremely high levels of greed and individualism unsustainable.

The tragedy of the commons is caused by short sightedness and selfishness. It explains a situation where individuals acting selfishly use up a shared resource even if it is clear that this is not in everyone's interest. The best-known example is where there is a shared piece of common ground, where everyone can graze their animals freely. Because it is free, some people take advantage of the opportunity by acquiring more animals. They seek to increase their own wealth at the expense of others. When only a few behave this way they get rich, while the socially responsible do not. It means that the under pricing of a resource, and the greed of a few, increases inequality. This is unjust, creating jealousy and social tension. It also encourages others to follow the example of the greedy. Eventually, when everyone behaves this way, it destroys the common good for everyone: so under pricing leads to the squandering and eventual loss of the resource. Everyone loses.

A modern-day example can be seen in the way the world's fishermen approach our wild fish stocks. The fishermen continue to fish the seas, even though it means they will eventually remove all the fish and their children will be unable to follow the same career. Today, around the world, trawlers sit idle because overfishing and the tragedy of the commons have depleted stocks.

As consumers, we do the same. We consume the world's wild fish stocks even though we know it will lead to the price of fish rising and their eventual eradication. We also know that it will mean there are no fish for future generations. The same greed and selfishness applies to the way we use much of the fresh water in the world, and non-renewable energy sources like coal, gas and oil. Humankind's desire to procreate so excessively is another example. We want children even though we know there are too many people in the world already. Thanks to a variety of policies, which limit the use of contraception and the availability of abortion in some countries, cheap food prices and a religious encouragement to breed, humanity has created its own global tragedy of the commons.

This does not make sense, certainly from any long-term perspective. Yet realizing that we have a problem is one thing, reversing the trend is another. When a culture of selfishness has grown and prospered, it is hard to turn the clock back. It is especially hard with our modern-day thinking about the world.

The freedom to behave as individuals, as well as the jealousy and greed inspired by the tragedy of the commons, encourages us to think less about society because we are told that we only need to think about ourselves.

The end result is the sort of opposition that US President Barack Obama faced with his healthcare reforms in 2010.

Many Americans believe that the poor should not have access to hospitals and medical care because they have not earned it. They do not think of healthcare as a right that should be available to all citizens. If the poor are given free medical care, the thinking goes, there would be less around for everyone else. Either that, or costs would go up and those who have worked to earn their medical coverage are worse off. In effect, those who are able to pay for healthcare would be forced to subsidize the poor. That, said Obama's opponents, is not what freedom, the free-market and individualism promise.

So withholding treatment from people when they are ill becomes an expression of freedom and individuality. Survival becomes a reward.

An exaggerated sense of self, without a responsibility to others, is not an ingredient of sustainable progress. It encourages waste and is a large part of the wider problems we face. Modern notions of individual freedom are at the root of our financial woes and our squandering of the world's resources.

But there is another way, and tiny Bhutan, a country with a population of less than 700,000 sandwiched between China and India, provides some food for thought.

Rather than measuring economic growth and encouraging citizens to think only about themselves, Bhutan attempts to measure GNH—Gross National Happiness. It believes, rightly, that the pursuit of economic growth without a well-embedded sense of social responsibility is not sustainable. Growth for its own sake is not in the best interests of the country's citizens.

Bhutan's government wisely says that using economic growth to measure progress robs children of their rightful share of the world's natural resources. Instead, the Bhutanese track nine indicators of progress including health, governance and psychological well-being. The components of the index "are a reflection of the kind of values my society upholds, the kind of values that we want to create, values of the real kind, wealth of the real kind, not of the illusory kind that can disappear overnight," says Bhutan's prime minister, Jigme Y. Thinley.

Bhutan is not alone. Thailand, the UK and Canada have started to think in a similar way, and in 2009 French President Nicolas Sarkozy asked two Nobel Prize winning economists, Joseph E. Stiglitz and Amartya Sen, to come up with a measure of progress that took into account the wider quality of life that citizens enjoy, the environment and education levels. Their report urged the world's leaders to drop their obsession with economic growth and use broader measures of prosperity instead.

To do so will require a different way of viewing the world. It will need people to think about each other again. It will need people to abandon the current notion of freedom and consider again the needs of those around them.

We all need a sense of social responsibility, especially if we are to tackle the challenges we face.

Endnote

1. US Census Bureau.

Part 2

Running Blind—We Are Poorly Equipped to Deal with These Challenges

---

Part one looked at many of the big challenges facing humankind. It looked at the way modern economic ideas and too little regulation brought about the 2007 financial crisis, the fallout from which will linger for years. It looked at the way the failures of new economic thinking have led us to under-price the world's resources, encouraging us to squander them. Continuing down this road is not sustainable. It looked at how we have changed our understanding of freedom, to create a greater sense of individualism. This change has brought more selfishness and greed, undermining our sense of social responsibility.

All of these changes in thinking have happened during the last few decades and are down to our abandoning or altering good Enlightenment principles.

Part two looks at how well we are equipped to address these challenges.

Chapter six looks at our levels of innovativeness and the state of the educational systems in much of the West. It is hard to find solutions to the problems we face if we are not thinking about the issues that should concern us.

Chapter seven looks at the ways our ideas of politics and government have changed. If we are to overcome the challenges which confront us, our governments will need to play a role. Yet they are not functioning correctly either. Instead of trying to build a better society, many of those in charge rule through fear, having privatized many of their most vital duties, and having transferred their power to big business.

Finally, we look at the implications of the rise of Asia, in particular China. When so many of our problems are due to abandoning, or watering down, of good principles, the rise of China promises to make the situation worse. Not only will we have to contend with a society that has an even greater hunger for instant rewards without considering the social costs, but fundamental notions of human rights are likely to wither too.

6

CAN YOU READ KANT?

Knowledge is power.

Sir Francis Bacon

Don't Start from Here

A journey depends on where you start. And this is not a good place to begin.

Many of the troubles humanity faces stem from the way we think about the world. In the last few decades we have undermined many of the principles we once had. This led to the financial crisis. It is causing us to waste the world's resources and it has resulted in a culture, in much of the world, which is driven by individual desires not a sense of social responsibility.

To address these troubles successfully means we need to think differently. Our current principles will not work. We need to find another set of guiding values with which to proceed, to work out where we want to go and why. We need a map.

Creating one, however, will be difficult. Few of us are thinking very deeply about the problems we face. Most of us are not thinking about them at all. In much of the developed world the cult of celebrity, the flood of trivia, and the belief that information is knowledge, is limiting our vision. The expectation of instant rewards without effort is undermining our sense of purpose.

Worse, a growing number of people are thinking in ways that will take us further in the wrong direction. In some parts of the world the rising influence of religion and a rediscovered mania for creationism are accelerating the shift of humanity backwards, to a time when science was scorned.

Moreover, changing attitudes and ideas is hard.

Enlightenment thinking was remarkable in the sense that it changed values without war or revolution, although it arguably led to both. It began the Age of Reason, shifting us beyond the confines of religious thinking that had dominated European civilization for centuries. Citizens, instead, began to think about science and logic, in fairness and the natural cycles of the world. It was a time when Western humankind was encouraged to lift itself above its daily struggles and to look forward to the development of a better world, a decent society. It was just the sort of transformation we need today.

The ideas of a few grew quickly, transforming the lives of thousands. Mathematicians, scientists, philosophers, lawyers, engineers and countless others started asking fundamental questions about the world. They put forward new ideas about justice, about property and the rights of individuals. They encouraged discourse and the flow of thoughts.

These ideas affected all of Western society. Across the Firth of Forth from where Smith was raised lies Edinburgh, in Scotland, where I was born. It was the home of Robert Louis Stephenson, author of *Treasure Island, Kidnapped* and the *Strange Case of Dr. Jekyll and Mr. Hyde.* Less well known is that Stephenson's grandfather, who was born a few years before Smith's *The Wealth of Nations* was published, and his father, were great men too. They are typical examples of how the world changed as a result of Enlightenment thinking. The elder Stephensons chose to use their engineering skills to help ships in trouble at sea. They saw this as a social duty. They wanted to find a means to prevent ships from running onto rocks and save lives. So they built many of the lighthouses that stand around Britain's coast today.

There are, of course, many comparable projects today, designed to improve the lives of humankind. The Large Hadron Collider, which has been built in Switzerland by the European Organization for Nuclear Research (CERN), is taking us into uncharted territory in particle physics. The International Thermonuclear Experimental Reactor (ITER) in France may generate power in the same way as the sun one day. Satellites have been sent to the farthest reaches of our solar system. Cracking the human genome has opened an encyclopedia of biological information for us to study.

But the ideas of modern economics are meddling here too. America's particle accelerator, Tevatron, will close in 2011 due to the budget cuts made necessary by the financial crisis. The free-market spirit has also affected the way we think about space travel. We are attempting to privatize much of it, while the US's National Aeronautics and Space Administration's (NASA) budget is being reduced. Most of America's technological spending actually goes towards weapons development, to keep another part of the economy in profit. We finished exploring most of the *terra firma* in our world 250 years ago but have only just started looking properly at the sea, the largest part. We still do not understand consciousness and know very little about what is in the universe around us. The sense of curiosity that was common during the Enlightenment now seems to fire only a few of us.

Despite giving the impression that we are living in an age of scientific wonder, our level of innovativeness has actually declined. According to Dr. Jonathan Huebner, a physicist working at the Pentagon's Naval Air Warfare Center in California, our rate of technological innovation peaked a century ago and has been declining ever since.

Huebner believes that the more minds there are, the more innovation there should be, all other things being equal. Yet, on this basis, the rate of technological progress we are making today is barely better than in the 1600s. The rate of innovation peaked in 1873 and has been declining ever since.[1] Extrapolating into the future, Huebner predicts that by 2024 our rate of innovation will drop to levels last seen in the Dark Ages.

According to Huebner, this is also partly because we have already found 85 percent of the fundamental technologies that are feasible. If science and technology were a tree, we have found the trunk and most of the branches already. There are very few important parts left to find. As with the "limits to growth" idea mentioned in chapter four, we are running up against limits with innovation.

Many of what we see as inventions today are only incremental improvements to products that have existed for decades.

We discovered DNA more than fifty years ago, prompting the genome project. The jet engine, the atom bomb, the silicon chip, the telephone and microwaves are all decades old.

In a history chronicling the last thirty years, how many of our inventions would be seen as major gains and how many would be seen simply as one- or two-step additions? We are not taking the steps that were as bold as those needed to discover gravity, new continents or the principles of flight.

That is not to say that innovation is over or that there will not be further change in the years ahead. It is simply to say there is evidence that the glory days for advancements of the sort needed to address the challenges we face are in the past. We are advancing in a flurry of incremental steps and this affects how we view the world.

Well, Duh!

One worrying potential reason for this is the fall in educational standards in many places, especially in the developed world. Despite students achieving steadily better grades in the US and UK, so much so that universities complain of having too many A-grade applicants, there is little to suggest that children are getting any smarter. More likely, subjects have been dumbed-down to make them more attractive and accessible.

For example, in the UK, a study by Michael Shayer of King's College London compared 800 secondary pupils in 2008 with their mid-1970s counterparts. He found the average fourteen-year-old today is better able to offer fast, quick-fire responses to questions. But he also found a lack of proper understanding, and an educational culture of learning that favored an instant, superficial way of handling information. "Everything in the past thirty years has speeded up. It's about reacting quickly but at a shallow level," he says. An earlier study, which compared the performance of present-day eleven- and twelve-year-olds with those taking the same test in the 1970s, found, simply, that standards had fallen.

A study by Oxford University's Department of Educational Studies and the Universities and Colleges Admissions Service in Britain found that students now show a lack independent thought and a fear of numbers. Britain's Confederation of British Industry and the Institute of Directors complain about declining standards of literacy and numeracy. A study by Sheffield University found that 17 percent of sixteen- to nineteen-year-olds were illiterate. They could not read or chart a course on a map. They could not understand a simple test with straightforward questions if there were distractions. Making inferences or understanding indirect meaning such as allusion or irony was either difficult for them or impossible. The study concluded that this is less than the level of literacy needed to hold a job, take part in family life and be a normal participative citizen.

For years, the US has dropped steadily down the league table of international education standards. Results from a comparative study[2] of 41 countries in 2009 showed US fourth-graders performed poorly and middle school students even worse. At the high school level, the US was near the bottom. In 2008, the US ranked twenty-first out of thirty OECD countries in scientific literacy,[3] with a quarter of American fifteen-year-olds unable even to meet the baseline level. In mathematics, the US ranked twenty-fifth, with almost 30 percent unable to demonstrate the kind of skills needed to use mathematics in daily life.

This weakening of educational standards is also a problem after students get to university. Courses have become much more modularized, broken into chunks of just a few weeks at a time. Because subjects are covered superficially, students only learn superficially.

James Côté, a professor of sociology at the University of Western Ontario and co-author of *Ivory Tower Blues: A University System in Crisis*, says that students today lack the linguistic skills to argue a case, are indiscriminate with source information and have a hard time focusing on a subject. Worse, they don't particularly care to improve, he says.

One reason for this change has been the drive to educate so many people. When nearly 50 percent of young people in the US and UK are expected to go to university, ten times the number that once went, there has been a coalescence around the mean levels that can be achieved.

One British sociologist, Frank Furedi, believes that intellectual life has been undermined by the pursuit of this drive for educational inclusion. He says that in their desire not to exclude anyone, universities have adopted policies that "flatter" students. "University lecturers are put under pressure to mark positively," he says. The situation has become so imbalanced that some academics fear being sued unless they provide "flattery instead of feedback."

Barely one-third of American children voluntarily read anything printed out of school today, down from 60 percent in 1982. Instead, they use their leisure time to watch television, listen to music, compose text messages, play video games and surf the Internet. Of course, some of this activity may be worthwhile. The Internet allows us easy access to vast quantities of valuable information. The question is: What is the quality and value of what is consumed?

Just as those who eat too often at fast-food restaurants tend to get fat and sick, those who consume information without thinking, tend to become mentally flabby too. It is not just that much of the information on the Internet is of dubious provenance, it is that much of what is posted as "fact" is actually opinion. Nor is it just the vacuousness of many television programs, it is also the levels of violence to which children are exposed. Studies in the US show that children will have seen about 8,000 murders[4] on average before the end of elementary school. They will also have watched about 20,000 adverts every year of their lives.

Partly as a result of this endless gorging on low-grade entertainment and consumption of media with shallow insight, almost one in three American children take no exercise and are overweight or obese. This is nearly triple the rate in 1963.[5] Too much television has lead to an increase in rates of depression, as well as sleep and behavioral problems.[6]

Finally, there is the opportunity cost. The time spent watching or playing a video game could have been spent doing something more productive.

In *The Dumbest Generation*, Mark Bauerlein says today's children are the dumbest ever, despite having unprecedented access to intellectual resources. He says most young people born since the mid-1980s in the US have been brought up on a diet of such weak educational standards, and a leisure time spent so fruitlessly, that they are unable to work alone reliably. Most never visit cultural institutions or take any interest in politics. They cannot explain basic scientific methods. Instead, they spend time passing stories, videos, music, and texts electronically between themselves and "dwelling in a world of puerile banter and coarse images. [On the Internet] they seek out what they already hope to find, and they want it fast and free, with a minimum of effort. Going online habituates them to juvenile mental habits."

Partly, this is the responsibility of a generation of parents who have indulged their children's wishes for fear of being labeled as curmudgeons. If Bauerlein is right, the consequences of their actions have not been thought through. A generation educated so poorly will be easy to manipulate, influence and control, either by those who develop and police social networking sites, by private companies seeking to profit from them, by governments that can act almost without recourse, and by those who present weak or biased data wishing to incite them to action.

When science is taught to such low standards, when there is a focus on process rather than knowledge, it becomes easier to displace enlightened ideas with those of religious babble. It is no coincidence that the rise in creationism and belief in faith-based medical treatment has occurred at a time when standards of scientific education have deteriorated.

The Internet is a particular problem. As well as offering a cozy home for factual mistakes or a platform for those with ill-thought-out opinions, there is the diversion it provides. Studies[7] show that people who read text that is scattered with hyperlinks understand less than those who read the old-fashioned printed word. Those who are continually distracted by emails and other messages understand less than those who are able to concentrate. People juggling many tasks tend to be less creative than those who focus. The Internet also encourages us to put more value on speed and group approval than on originality and creativity.

In his excellent book, *The Shallows: What the Internet is Doing to Our Brains,* Nicholas Carr says there is evidence that the Internet is even damaging long-term memory consolidation, which is the basis for true intelligence. We spend an average of fifty-six seconds[8] on each web page and all this clicking, skipping and skimming seems to be having an effect on deep memory.

Michael Merzenich, a neuroscientist at the University of California in San Francisco, believes our brains are being "massively remodeled" through this process. He is profoundly worried about the long term consequences of the distractions and interruptions of the Internet. He frets that we will lose our capacity to engage in contemplation, reflection and introspection. Because the Internet scatters our thoughts we risk losing the ability to focus on issues of importance, such as where humanity is heading.

There is, of course, another factor at play here that we need to consider. It is that the approach we are taking to education today is no longer appropriate for the world we live in: the model we use is wrong. Most of the Western educational systems are still based, ironically, in the time of the Enlightenment and the Industrial Revolution. Learning is seen as a staged process, with the goal of taking young children and turning them into young adults who can get jobs. For decades that system seemed to make sense. But it is not entirely clear that it is still right for today. The world we live in is very different. Jobs do not follow schooling automatically; careers are not for life. Moreover, it is not the fault of our children that they have to contend with so many distractions—so much that is opinion and not fact—on the Internet.

The problem is not really that humanity is getting dumber. After all, we are still genetically much the same as we were hundreds of generations ago. The problem is that we are not producing citizens who are able to contemplate and consider properly the problems we face.

Going My Way?

Either because of poorer standards of education or inappropriate ones, we are moving backwards intellectually. In the absence of any clear moral or political philosophy beyond individualism, the free market and consumption, without a comprehensive view of the world, based on reliable sources of information, in a world where fact and opinion are merged as entertainment, most of us are left to form ideas using scraps of information with varying degrees of validity. We risk moving towards an "Age of Philistinism," with a widespread desire for wealth and material possessions, but with little interest in ethics or in what is right. We face a world of smug ignorance and conventionalism.

These concerns are already being reflected in many Western political systems. America's Tea Party movement, which wants to return to conservative ideas based loosely around the notion of patriotism, is a good example. Claiming to be morally superior is a useful tactic when struggling for political power, but when such claims also depend only on blind faith, self interest, or misguided idealism, they risk taking the country in the wrong direction.

In 1869 Mill wrote about the "tyranny of the majority," a fate to which democracies are prone. Once the majority have control they use their power to suppress the ideas of the minority and so control everyone. This can lead to dangerous laws being passed and the emergence of a political elite who can wield enormous power—as happened in Russia in the 1920s and Germany in the 1930s. When the majority are indifferent, or do not understand the implications of what they are voting for, this risk rises.

In the US and elsewhere, political conservatives are becoming increasingly forceful in their efforts to encourage a return to traditional values, both through the Tea Party movement and with Christian evangelism. They see their ideas responding to a need for greater social cohesion.

Yet, their actions threaten to bring greater social division instead, undermining much of what has been achieved in the last few centuries. The return to theocratic societies throws away years of scientific and social progress, encouraging people to adopt outdated and oppressive ideas that constrain social and scientific development. There is a risk of rising hostility between conflicting fundamental beliefs, a bipolar perspective of right and wrong, of good and evil, of one religion against another, which incites conflict.

China is one among the few countries that have had the courage to voice concerns about where culture and society are heading intellectually. The president, Hu Jintao, has lashed out at the media for producing material which is vulgar and kitsch, and which encourages excessive consumerism. Cai Wu, the culture minister, has railed against publications that are full of gossip, that encourage vanity and the worship of money, comparing the poor standard of books published today with those of China's glorious history.

Their existence, he said, was the result of China's move towards a free-market economy, to the polluting power of a *laissez-faire* approach to cultural development.

Perhaps he has a point.

Despite students achieving better grades, there has been a lowering of thinking skills across much of the world. Given our challenges this is at best unhelpful and at worst a hindrance. If we are to find a way to fix our problems we will need to reverse this trend. We will need to find a way to elevate people's thoughts again, to shift humanity off its current path.

Once we have done that, once we know what we want, we can begin to move in a better direction. All we will need then is the political process to make the necessary changes. We will need those in charge to apply the principles we want to live by, to regulate and govern the needs of society as we define them.

Unfortunately there is a problem here too.

Endnotes

1. "A possible declining trend for worldwide innovation," *Technological Forecasting and Social Change*, Jonathan Huebner 2005.
2. Third International Mathematics and Science Study (TIMSS) 2009.
3. Alliance for Educational Excellence, Washington, Fact Sheet March 2008.
4. Compiled by TV-Free America, see http://www.csun.edu/science/health/docs/tv&health.html, Article "Television and Health" by Dr. Norman Herr. Statistics from AV Nielsen study.
5. Report, "Understanding Childhood Obesity," 2010, American Heart Association Page 1.
6. "Children's Television Exposure and Behavioral and Social Outcomes at 5.5 Years: Does Timing of Exposure Matter?" American Academy of Pediatrics, October 2007.
7. Clifford Nass, Stanford University's Communication Between Humans and Interactive Media Lab studies. The lab works on experimental studies of social-psychological aspects of human-computer interaction. See also "Does the Internet Make You Dumber?", *WSJ* article by Nicolas Carr, June 5, 2010.
8. AC Neilsen. "Does the Internet Make You Dumber?", *WSJ* article by Nicolas Carr, June 5, 2010.

7

WHO IS IN CHARGE?

A government, for protecting business only, is but a carcass, and soon falls by its own corruption and decay.

Amos Bronson Alcott

Someone Needs to Make Decisions

It may be the most foolish idea put forward by those on the outlying fringes of America's Republican Tea Party movement. Their suggestion that we do not need any form of democratic government is not merely irresponsible, it is dangerous, even if it has growing popular support. We may need less government, but we are unlikely to survive very long without any at all.

Indeed, given the complexity of the challenges we face, we probably need more government. It is how and where this should be provided that is the more difficult question to answer.

During the last thirty years the influence of many national governments has shrunk, especially in the West. Increased personal, financial and corporate mobility as well as technological changes have made it harder for governments to govern as they once did. The richest people and the biggest companies, which would normally pay the most taxes, are much freer to move to where the fiscal and legislative burden suits them best. Financially, many businesses have also become many times bigger than the governments that nominally attempt to regulate them.

Socially, citizens have changed the way they relate to each other too. Once regulatory authorities were expected to govern groups of close-knit communities, people who shared similar values and objectives. Today, many of us have more in common—and more contact—with people on other continents than we do with our immediate neighbors. We see less justification for national or even local authorities.

Governments also find themselves increasingly in competition with each other. Once, the rivalry was mostly about power, trade and international influence. Now it also includes competing with regulations; about who can have the weakest laws to attract the most inward investment. The welfare of local citizens and tax payers often takes second place to the demands of big business.

National authorities also face more of a regulatory dilemma than in the past. They have an increasing need to legislate on issues that are outside their traditional sphere of influence. Many business sectors act globally, while the legislative options open to governments remain mostly local. This imbalance was one of the biggest dilemmas facing bank regulators after the 2007 financial crisis.

With so many unsettling forces, many have started to question whether the concept of the nation state is now dead.

It may be. But in a world where we badly need to find answers to the very large problems that we face, another conclusion is also clear. Someone needs to be in charge. Humankind needs to make decisions if it is to avoid another financial crisis and responsibly manage what remains of the world's resources. Implementing changes to the way we approach the world will need wisdom, strength and diplomacy. These are not issues that can be addressed by those who have had their head turned by the notion of untrammeled individualism. That would be a recipe for disaster.

So we are in an odd place. Although we do not have an alternative to national government that works, or is even being seriously proposed, the value and purpose of what we currently have is disintegrating. Yet we also have a need for change, to move in another direction.

There is a gap and for now the vacuum is being filled by politicians who are less interested in the big challenges we face and more interested in retaining power. So they increasingly rule by fear. The space is also being filled by large corporations, unelected powers interested in profit rather than our well-being.

As a result, we are in danger of making a bad situation even worse.

Nothing Is Terrible Except Fear Itself

Billions of citizens in the world are being made to worry. Instead of being encouraged to consider the well-being of each other, or how we might build a better world, they are inspired, instead, to fret about the threat of war, terrorism, food shortages and climate change.

Much of this fear is real, of course. Humankind really does risk running out of water and oil and many other items essential to our lives. The risk of terrorism is greater than it has been for decades too, thanks greatly to the actions of inept Western politicians. There are also serious threats from the effects of climate change.

But rather than persuading us to respond positively to these challenges, rather than inspiring us to step up to the task, we are made to sit back and worry while those in government treat the symptoms rather than the causes. Without any meaningful political philosophy, politicians around much of the world have latched on to an age-old tool to control their citizens—fear. So they inflate the risks to keep their jobs.

The concept of ruling this way is as ancient as humanity. As Nicolò Machiavelli said 500 years ago: it is safer for a ruler to be feared than loved.[1]

Thirty years ago, Western politicians encouraged their citizens to fear the Soviet Union. They told tales about the thousands of missiles that had been stockpiled, wildly inflating the threat. More recently, the threat was the imaginary Iraqi weapons of mass destruction. Now it is al-Qaeda, an organization that is to a great extent a construct of the US's Central Intelligence Agency (CIA).

Today's politicians have also encouraged divisions between the peoples of the world, although perhaps less deliberately. In almost every country, they have promoted unsustainable economic development, they have handed control of many of the world's resources to private companies, and they have sat passively while standards of dialogue and debate about the challenges we face have deteriorated.

They have supported a system that has enabled the rich to get richer, thereby increasing society's inequality. They have even pushed back civil liberties and human rights. US politicians have even introduced military tribunals, a violation of the 6th Amendment, and mass detentions without trial, in violation of the 5th.

Man Is Born Free but Everywhere Is in Chains

The fear used to manage our world has been achieved by gradual and stealthy means. It helps, of course, that many of those living in the West have been "dumbed-down." It is easier when many people are no longer thinking about the big issues that should concern them. Relevant facts are sometimes manipulated or withheld from us, as with the fabricated evidence about Iraq's weapons of mass destruction. Emotive words are also used by many Western politicians for added tension: some examples are the Axis of Evil and the War on Terror. The word "terrorist" is applied liberally, almost without thought. Every freedom fighter is now a terrorist, while voices that call for major political change are labeled a threat. Minorities are stigmatized, as are, for example, many Muslims living in the West today—mirroring what happened to minority groups in Germany in the 1930s. North Korea's plans for its defense, Iran's plans to build a nuclear power plant, Palestinian attempts to protect their land, the Taliban's bombs in Afghanistan, as well as bombers in Ireland, or rebels in Africa, are all grouped together as sources of terror, as if the people behind them all have the same agenda.

Many Western politicians are also restricting our liberty.

Liberty seems an easy notion to understand. Originally it meant freedom from tyranny. There was liberty in being protected from decisions made at the whim of a landowner. It meant freedom from slavery. As society developed, the word began to mean more. At a political level, it gradually came to mean that the rulers of a country became its servants. In most Western societies, the kings and queens were replaced by democratically elected representatives who, in theory at least, served the needs of their electorate. Each person was at liberty to cast a vote and through that freedom all people were able to choose the form of government they wanted.

During the last thirty years, the balance of power has shifted away from the electorate and towards those in power. It is not just Mill's notion of the tyranny of the majority we face today, whereby the voices of the minority are often silenced. We also face the tyranny of those in power. Politicians are inflicting their will on those they are supposed to represent, stifling dissent and suppressing the freedom of individuals.

More than 200 years ago Jean-Jacques Rousseau fought against such restrictions. Rousseau believed that individuals and civil authority need to act in harmony, that each has moral obligations towards the other. Political authority is based on a fair and just agreement among the members of a society. A government must protect the rights, liberty and equality of its citizens or it breaks the social contract that lies at the heart of political authority.

Yet the social contract in America, much of Europe and Asia has been broken. Private discussions and the movement of people are monitored, while governments insist on secrecy for their own actions, as new laws and systems are created to limit their citizens' freedoms.

John Locke said that if a government violates the rights of its citizens, the people can legitimately rebel. Such thoughts did much to inspire the ideals of the French and American Revolutions. Locke helped inspire Thomas Paine's ideas about revolution and influenced many other founders of modern America including Benjamin Franklin and Thomas Jefferson.

When the US was attacked on September 11, 2001 (9/11), the president at the time, George W. Bush, said that the Middle-Eastern terrorists had been motivated by a simple notion. It was, he said, "because we love freedom and they hate freedom."

This was a curious statement, not just because it was clearly nonsense.

The terrorists did not hate freedom. Like anyone else, they hated repression and injustice. They saw Middle-Eastern countries being bullied into adopting an economic model that they did not want. They saw their oil reserves being plundered to fuel the West's cars and trucks. They saw they were being poorly paid for their oil and that their citizens would one day face dwindling supplies and an uncertain economic future. They saw the West invading Iraq and its meddling in the affairs of other sovereign states in the region, including those of Saudi Arabia, Egypt, Iran, Afghanistan and Pakistan. They felt that Islam and the rights of Muslims were being trampled on.

In all this, they were right. Whatever the terrorists were trying to achieve, they were not acting against the notion of liberty.

Moreover, the very freedoms Bush was so proud of are now being restricted. The US *PATRIOT Act*, (its full title is *Uniting and Strengthening America by Providing Appropriate Tools Required to Intercept and Obstruct Terrorism Act* of 2001, commonly known just as the Patriot Act) several anti-terrorism acts in the UK, and similar legislation in other European countries and Australia, undermine liberty. The Patriot Act gives the US government the right to monitor anyone directly or electronically as long as it can show that the information collected is relevant to an ongoing criminal investigation.[2] It can obtain the source and addressee information of all telephone and online communications and gain access to unopened electronic mail. Internet service providers and banks are required to disclose records to the Federal Bureau of Investigation (FBI) when asked. In the UK, the presumption of innocence has been effectively abolished.[3] In both the UK and US, the state can also collect DNA samples, even from those not convicted of any crime.

During the Enlightenment such events would have been unthinkable. It would have been unimaginable that private letters between individuals could be opened and read by the state automatically. Yet e-mails and texts are now filtered and monitored in most countries. This is done in the name of security, to protect us from the fear that the politicians have exploited and inflated. It would have been inconceivable even thirty years ago for Western governments to demand unrestricted access to medical, financial, business, and educational records. They could not authorize secret searches of homes and offices without considerable legal process. Yet these are permitted in America.[4]

Today's laws might seem reasonable when it comes to targeting and capturing terrorists or in responding to atrocities such as 9/11. But the authorities are also undermining the liberty and privacy of all decent citizens, creating a sense of injustice and distrust. For the *possible* actions of a few hundred people, 330 million Americans and just as many Europeans are being spied on. They still have free speech. But the state is watching, reading and listening to what they say.

Combined with social trends on the Internet, the overall result is a curious one. On one side, the state in many countries is becoming more oppressive, limiting liberty and cutting off basic rights. People can be kidnapped abroad and imprisoned in America or third countries without trial, so long as they are deemed dangerous to US security. Ironically, the fundamental right to *habeas corpus* is being restricted in the name of freedom. Some people who have been detained in Guantanamo since 2002 will now be held for life without trial, although they may not have committed any act that would "constitute a chargeable offense in either a federal court or military commission."[5]

There is no greater signal of tyranny than a government throwing a person into prison for life at the whim of an executive without any sort of impartial review.

At the same time, many people are becoming more open about their ideas and lives, happily publishing photographs of themselves taking drugs or revealing their innermost thoughts online. Few seem concerned.

Yet they should be, for much of what they hand over carries risks, perhaps not today, but in the future.

In Europe, the US or Asia, the technology channels carrying these personal insights are dominated by just a handful of private companies. In operating systems, motherboard chipsets, chat software, social networking programs and search engines, a tiny number of providers are in control. Intel, Skype, Apple, Google, Amazon, Microsoft, Facebook and Twitter have all entered the dictionary because they are near-monopoly providers—globally.

Smith was very clear about monopoly power. He called it a great enemy. He believed that monopolies are bad for markets and bad for society. He advocated regulatory intervention to control them.

It is easy to see why.

What these companies do with the information they have about us remains largely unregulated—even though many have already demonstrated questionable ethical standards. Skype can be used to spy on users' phone calls. Facebook keeps running up against privacy action groups and says it wants to achieve "world domination." The chips inside most mobile phones can listen in to what we say. Microsoft and Apple know what software we install. Like Intel, Microsoft has been fined for anticompetitive behavior. Apple is accused of it. Google tracks where we go on the Internet and is scanning the world's libraries into a database. This might seem laudable: we will be able to access books that are rare or hard to find. Except Google has never said it is doing this for charity. Soon, a privately held monopoly will control access to most of the world's digitized books.

Moreover, as search engine companies filter what they put out, how can China, Russia and many Arab nations, among others, ensure that they are properly heard? So much of the news we receive about them flows through pipelines which are now controlled by these private American companies. Who decides what comes out the other end? Who will control it tomorrow? If Google was Chinese, Russian or Iranian citizens in the West would be outraged, demanding change. Instead they remain sanguine, confident that their own technology companies are looking after their best interests, without considering any mechanisms to regulate what is going on.

It may not always be sufficient simply to believe they will not "be evil." For those who lived in Herbert Hoover's America, in the Soviet Union during the 1960s, in East Germany in the 1980s, or in China during the late 1960s, such openness makes for unease. Being open about political ideas, about sexual preferences or about the use of drugs is still dangerous in many countries.

Don't bloggers and social networkers ever consider the power they transfer to others by their activities? Do they not know that they can be easily traced? Do they imagine that the managers of the businesses that host their rants will never choose to exercise their influence? Do they think that the world described by

George Orwell in *1984* or the politics of totalitarianism are simply old ideas from the past?

Who declared them dead?

Who Is in Charge?

At the root of these challenges lie questions about who is in charge—and who should be in charge. Is it the politicians, with their scaremongering? Is it big business, with its global reach, financial power and ability to side-step national regulations? Or do we need something else, something new?

Part of the problem in many Western societies is that government has, in a sense, been privatized. Getting elected in the US and many other countries requires spending millions of dollars on the political campaign. The 2012 presidential election is predicted to be the first to cost more than $1 billion.

Such hefty expenditures mean that the rich get into public office more easily than the poor. In office, politicians have the opportunity and sometimes the obligation to direct spending to support those who backed them, ignoring the needs of wider society. Even for honest politicians, for those who avoid the ample opportunities for personal gain through taking office, there is the chance to cash-in later. Once they are out of office, they can sit on boards or make a fortune from the speaker circuit. For many politicians, getting elected is about serving their own needs, not the needs of society.

Smith also hated lobbyists because of the risk that they would cloud the judgment of even the purist of social thinkers. Yet in America, today, the gun lobby as well as those who support many other industrial groups are immensely successful in persuading politicians to act in their favor, even where there is clear evidence that the decisions made or laws passed as a result of their activities are not always in the interests of the majority of citizens. There is even a lobby group in the US, the Center for Consumer Freedom, which is backed by the food industry to promote "free choice" in food. It encourages people to eat sugary, fatty, salty foods in the name of freedom, despite the health risks and costs to society that result.

These groups and the politicians who respond to them are gaining from wrong-headedness. They undermine good government. They promote policies that favor a few and harm many. These businesses lobby to make a profit. The policies that result damage society, increasing healthcare costs, pollution, ill health and crime.

Both the business heads and the politicians justify their actions by persuading their citizens that this is democracy; that this is what liberty and freedom provide. People are free to choose, they say, even if they then choose wrongly, and in the interests of the profiteers.

It was not always like this. Politicians (although not all of them) were once much more motivated to serve, to meet the needs of the people. French Enlightenment politicians sought a system that promoted reason, tolerance and social progress. Of course, the politics then did not always lead to the intended consequences—sometimes causing wars and revolutions. But, at least, the politicians of the time were guided by principles of justice and fairness, of equality and nature. They were less motivated by ideas of profit or swayed by the pressures of private enterprise.

For decades there has been a global struggle between the parties of left and right, between socialism and the free-market libertarians. With the fall of the Berlin Wall, many in the Western world seem to have concluded that this struggle is over. The free market won. As a result, it is hard to distinguish the politicians of the Left and Right in much of Europe or America today. Their ideas are not based on concepts of capital or labor as they once were, but on nuances of how to maintain the *status quo*. Even in supposedly communist countries such as China and Russia, equality has given way to individual greed too, despite the same dominant party remaining in power. Income distribution in these countries has become polarized again.

Thomas Jefferson believed that politicians needed to show "decent respect for the opinions of mankind." Yet, such ideas have been largely forgotten. In most of the world, politicians have become disengaged from the societies they represent. They focus on retaining power, thinking about the present more than the future. They emphasize the vulnerabilities of their citizens and see any radical opposition to their ideas as a problem to be managed. Politics and government should not be like this.

We need good government. We need to reverse this tide of political "endarkenment."

Endnotes

1. Niccolò di Bernardo dei Machiavelli, *The Prince*, 1532, Chapter 17, first page.
2. "The Impact of the Patriot Act on Employers," Rothgerber, Johnson and Lyons, LLP, January 2003.
3. Liberty's Briefing to the House of Commons on the draft Prevention of Terrorism Act 2005 (Continuance in force of sections 1 to 9) Order 2010.
4. "The Impact of the Patriot Act on Employers," Rothgerber, Johnson and Lyons, LLP, January 2003.
5. Final Report, President Obama's Guantanamo Review Task Force, January 22, 2010, *Washington Post*, May 28, 2010.

8

CHINA'S RISING INFLUENCE WILL NOT HELP

I wouldn't mind seeing China if I could come back the same day.

Philip Larkin, English poet

It Can Get Worse

The Western economic and political value system, which is at the heart of so many our global problems, faces another challenge that is likely to undermine many remaining enlightenment ideas further still.

During the next twenty years, unless there is some cataclysmic economic, climactic or political change, the influence, ideas and values of Chinese society will rise. China will spread its political wings, demanding a greater say in important global decisions. Tourism will bring hundreds of millions of Chinese people and their customs to far-off lands. Chinese companies will build an international presence, bringing their business practices and values with them.

Yet China's attitudes to human rights, privacy, meritocracy, law and order, labor, democracy, money making and the environment are often in direct conflict with those of Western societies.

As the West's economic power begins to wane, as its share of the world's economy diminishes, its centuries-old sense of moral superiority will be confronted by a set of principles that are not just alien, but run counter to many long-held beliefs.

There will be a clash of values at a time when it will be even harder for the West to argue that its liberalized free-market, democratic model is best.

Chinese ideas about how societies should function will become stronger, affecting people in the West in ways that few can probably imagine.

The Dragon Is Awake

If it stays on its current path, China will become the world's biggest economy in about fifteen years. From being an agrarian-based, almost feudal society in the 1980s, China has become the fastest moving economic force in the world in the last twenty-five years, shifting from pre- to post-industrial in not much more than an evolutionary blink. Although it accounted for less than 10 percent of world GDP in 2010, it is already one of the biggest consumers of raw materials and the biggest user of energy. It is home to some of the world's largest banks. And it is where the rise of consumerism and materialism has been fastest.

Yet China's path to American-style levels of development will become harder. As the world's resource shortages begin to take effect, it will have to battle with the developed world for the raw materials that remain. How the country and its citizens handle this challenge will affect us all.

China's most cherished philosophies are fundamentally different from those of post-Enlightenment societies. Chinese societies[1] are generally based on Confucian-derived ideas of filial piety (respect for parents and ancestors), respect for authority, a strong work ethic, a desire for education and thrift.

Confucian principles view the hierarchy of peoples differently. Chinese loyalty is first to parents, then the clan and the state. The notion of promoting staff in a company based on merit, for example, runs counter to a system that prefers to protect the interests of a family or well-established social group. Law and order is not the same as in the West either, because the State retains absolute control. Animal welfare or concerns for the environment are viewed through a different philosophical prism too. Instead of feeling a sense of responsibility for the planet, Chinese societies see the world and other species, which are further down the natural hierarchy of life, as a source of opportunity. The recent increase in environmental legislation in China is not because Beijing wants to protect the planet. It is because rising pollution and cancer levels are threatening social stability. Environmental challenges are also viewed positively because they offer a business opportunity.

Chinese societies do not think about "rights" the way the West does. They do not seek to protect individual or human rights. There are no rights to privacy and property rights are generally weaker. Chinese-dominated Asian countries are actually distrustful of notions of individual freedom and political liberalism, preferring to emphasize order and discipline instead. Individuals are expected to sacrifice Western concepts of freedom, including freedom of expression or freedom to congregate, for the good of society. Such ideas are sometimes used to justify authoritarian or paternalistic political systems and are reflected in work practices, employee rights and working hours. Governments in the region defend this lack of individual freedom by saying simply that their system works—it is a foundation of their rapid economic growth. This means that there is little interest in Western notions of democracy—because they do not fit with Confucian ideas of stability, harmony and control.

The United Nations (UN) Declaration of Human Rights states that individuals are born free and equal. It reflects the Enlightenment notions of freedom and democracy. The Declaration also says that people have a right not to be discriminated against on the basis of color, sex, language, religion, political or other opinion, national or social origin, property, birth or other status. They have a right to life and liberty. They must not be tortured or treated cruelly. Each person is equal before the law. They should have the right to work, to leisure, the right to clothing and shelter, the right to education and the right to healthcare.

While they are not alone, the governments and citizens of East-Asian nations view many of these notions as soft-headed nonsense—the products of warped post-imperialist minds.

In Chinese-based societies, the idea that people have a "right" to work, a "right" to leisure and a "right" not to be arbitrarily deprived of their property makes no sense at all. In these countries individuals are not free, in the Western sense. They are answerable to the hierarchy.

Making staff work sixteen-hour days, seven days a week, without any time off is not something that would keep a Chinese boss awake at night. If someone's house is sited in the way of a new road or the mayor's next house, then it is the house owner's problem, not the state's. If the state cannot remove a citizen's house when it needs to, how can society progress? How can the needs of the majority be properly served if one person's voice is allowed to hinder the majority's needs?

Of Privileges and Principles

Despite these differences, Chinese and Western societies appear, superficially, to have been following the same path during the last twenty years. The growth in consumption and the ability of individuals to act as they wish have become much more important in China, as well as in the West.

Yet the paths and starting points are different. In the West, the rise in consumption has come at the cost of many traditional values. Ideas of equality and social responsibility have been tarnished by the process.

In China, and many other Asian countries, consumption has actually reinforced important traditional ideas. Centuries-old principles of hard work and thrift have become more closely intertwined with materialism. Conspicuous consumption has become a vital symbol of achievement, visible proof of hard work and thrift. In China, materialism actually results in a greater sense of well-being and higher self-esteem. Unlike in the West, where years of rising consumption have brought no net gain in happiness, materialism in Chinese societies has provided that all-important sense of "face." It has been a source of great happiness, at least for those who have become richer.

This is why companies selling branded clothes, luxury cars, fancy watches, expensive brandy and French handbags are so successful in Asia. Conspicuous consumption lets people show what they have achieved. Even the dead are given Rolex watches, gold bars, the keys to a Mercedes and expensive designer clothes, at least in the form of paper offerings. Chinese people reflect their "self" through their material possessions. The more lavish and expensive the item, the more successful the individual must be. A $10,000 bottle of Château Lafite makes a powerful statement to friends and colleagues. Pouring into the ashtray to extinguish the embers of the last Cuban cigar makes an even more powerful statement. It signifies the sort of wealth that is so great that such waste is a trifle. That kind of action gains great respect.

Moreover, the goods Chinese people buy must be new and real. Second-hand items, which are infused with the previous owner's questionable fate, or counterfeits, are not sufficient, despite the widespread sale of fakes in Asia.

In the West, people tend to think about working less when they have achieved sufficient levels of wealth to be able to live better. They will trade riches tomorrow for comfort today. They take more vacation time to relax. Such notions barely exist in Chinese culture. There is much less of a sense of "enough" when it comes to the acquisition of "bling." There is always the potential to achieve more, and to not pursue it is a betrayal of Chinese values. Not working when you are able is a sign of laziness. It reduces self esteem. As author Arthur Rosenfeld puts it:[2]

> While the recent recession has many Americans rethinking the wisdom of chasing money and things all our life even at the cost of our health and happiness, the Chinese have no such reservations. Theirs is an all out frenzy of industry, a rampant desire to assume economic primacy in the world. . . . Stripped of their august cultural heritage by the brutality of the Cultural Revolution, the Chinese seem to be in a headlong rush to what they think they want and need—the material excess of the West—and are zooming forward without either social restraint or the lessons of history in place.

In the 1980s, when Deng Xiaoping was "paramount leader," China was a very equal place. Wealth was more evenly distributed than in almost any other country in the world. The Gini coefficient (see chapter five) was below 20.

As a result of the rapid pursuit of wealth during the last twenty years, it has become increasingly polarized. In 2009, the top 10 percent of China's population—140 million people—controlled almost half the country's riches with the remaining 1.3 billion people torn between wanting to mimic them or rebel against their excesses.

This rising tide of wealth, materialism and consumption is important to all of us. It affects how Chinese-based cultures view the world's resources and provide a focus for their ambitions. If we look for ways to price the world's resources properly, or break the cycle of cost externalization in the coming years, China will need to play a part too. It will account for much of the growth in the world—and most of the consumption growth. If Chinese views oppose any attempts at rebalancing, if they are in favor of ever more consumption and are unconcerned about widening income inequalities in society, the job will be much harder.

These differences in philosophy have also made it hard for many foreign companies to do business in China. This has not put millions of them off, however, and much continues to be written about their adventures. For the last twenty years China has seemed like the answer to a prayer. Just as demand for almost everything began to wane in Europe and America, China with its 1.4 billion people, rising wealth and hunger for consumer goods, was a wish come true.

In practice, however, few business people have thought very deeply about why they invested in China. Few bothered to understand the society, its values or the nature of the challenges they would face. They invested because they thought it would become a big market for their products one day; they invested because their rivals went there; because they thought they could find low-cost labor, or because their shareholders believed a presence in China was essential.

Most bosses in Europe or the US with subsidiaries in China visit the country a couple of times every year and think they have made a wise decision. They fly to Shanghai, take the world's fastest train into the city center, meet with their colleagues in a smart, modern skyscraper, have a world-class dinner overlooking the famous Bund and then fly back to base feeling quietly self-satisfied. Although they hear noises about corruption, shoddy quality and counterfeiting, they see a business and a country powering ahead. The stock markets like the fact their company is investing there. It does not even matter if their business is still unprofitable because, they reason, the returns will come in the long term.

To get another view, they should speak to those at the "coal-face," those foreigners who have worked in China for years, be they Westerners or those of Chinese descent from Singapore, Hong Kong and Taiwan.

They tell very different stories. They talk of "shifting legal sands"—where the laws keep changing. They talk of systematic theft of information and assets, with 98 percent of foreign companies in China reporting fraudulent activities and data theft.[3] They tell stories about long-term strategies orchestrated by local and national governments and their "partners" to squeeze them out. They talk of rampant corruption, high staff turnover and the problems of finding reliable managers. Many have experience working in other Asian countries. And they will tell you that China is different. The scale and extent of the problems foreign businesses encounter are on a much more substantial scale than elsewhere.

There is an expression in Shanghai, "we can copy everything except your mother," because almost everything can be duplicated. There are fake hotels, which use the names of international chains, fake network routers, known as Chiscos, and fake cars, which are sometimes copied from the drawings of rivals and appear on the roads before the "original." In hospitals, patients risk being given fake blood plasma. Those in business will find their employees submit fake receipts for expenses and apply for jobs with fake references and fake degrees. Some of the best educated will claim they are the authors of worthy scientific papers, although the findings will have been faked or plagiarized. If applicants achieved good marks in exams, someone else may have written the paper for them, or their parents may have paid teachers to give them the answers. In the prestigious civil service exams about 250 people are caught cheating every month.[4] There are fake banks lending to the black market, and fake fruit injected with dubious fluids to look firm and ripe. There are even fake contestants. In the 2010 Xiamen marathon, thirty runners were caught cheating, hiring *doppelgängers* to run much of the route before a car deposited them near the finishing line to run the last few hundred meters.

It is common practice for secretaries in China to be paid a "commission" by travel agents when they book flights for their bosses. Receptionists can be financially enticed to refer sales enquiries to competitors. Employees can form groups to exploit an employer and share the profits they make.

Similarly, business managers will happily make transfers of assets to themselves or companies in which they have a stake. They will falsify accounts or set up competing businesses. This is because, in the hierarchy, their loyalty is first to their family and trusted friends, not the company that employs them.

While all this may be shocking to China novices or to those who failed to understand the market before investing, these practices are not new. They have been characteristics of doing business in China since the time of Confucius. The foreign investors should have known that this was the way things worked before they invested.

What is of great concern now, however, is the push by Chinese companies to expand overseas. For Western companies to face such challenges in China is one thing; to have to face them in other markets as well, or even at home, is quite another.

There Is Anger Too

More troubling still, for those in Japan and the West, there are strong emotions running through the minds of many Chinese people when they venture abroad. There is a sense of anger about past injustices committed by the West and Japan and a desire for these wrongs to be righted.

China may no longer be a land of Maoist leftists waving *Little Red Books* and calling for the destruction of the Western capitalist system. But a strong and dangerous enmity towards much of the outside world remains. This needs to be added to the Chinese-values cocktail that Western societies are about to consume in ever greater quantities. They may find it leaves a bitter taste.

During the Mao years, Chinese school books were written with what was called a "victory narrative."[5] Children were taught that the Communist Party of China was the party of victory because it had won wars against the Nationalists (who retreated and took government in Taiwan), the Americans and the Japanese.

After the Tiananmen Square massacre in 1989, however, the emphasis changed. A new "patriotic education campaign" portrayed China not as a victor over its enemies, but as a victim of foreign abuse. Since 1992, school books have been modified to reflect this view and history about the country's "national humiliation" has been made compulsory. The Communist Party is now seen as the party of national salvation.

Official documents, history books and popular culture have also been changed. In the mid-1990s the government launched a propaganda campaign to evoke memories of the "hundred years of humiliation," which began with the Opium War in 1840. Citizens were also reminded of the war against Japan, the Rape of Nanjing in 1937–38, and the role America played in supporting the Communist Party's nationalist rivals. The Central Propaganda Department identified 100 national, historic sites that would receive financial support to get the message across. Some of these were battlefields and monuments in memory of patriotic martyrs, while others reflected China's ancient civilization. Visits to the sites were organized for school children, army personnel and government officials. Provinces were encouraged to identify their own historical sites and deepen the process of patriotic education further. Of the forty sites devoted to foreign invasions, half focused on the war with Japan.

In the decade following the Tiananmen Square massacre, a nation was taught that it had been a victim of injustice, that foreigners, especially the Japanese, Americans and Europeans, had wronged them.

This patriotic education campaign remains in force. In 2004, new guidelines were issued to "liberate thoughts," especially of the young. The Communist Party introduced a new patriotic project, "The Three One Hundred for Patriotic Education" campaign. Seven ministries, including the Ministry of Education and the Propaganda Department, recommended 100 films, 100 songs, and 100 books. Financial support was provided for their distribution. One of the books was entitled *Never Forget Our National Humiliation*, while one of the films highlighted a battle between Chinese and

American troops during the Korean War. In 2005, many of the historical sites identified in the 1990s campaign were relaunched under a domestic tourism drive.

For many Chinese today, there remains a patriotic desire to right the perceived (and real) wrongs of the past meted out by foreigners. This sense will underpin China's approach to its integration with the world in the decades to come.

A bestselling book, *Unhappy China—The Great Time, Grand Vision and Our Challenges*, is stirring debate in China and alarm in the West because of its aggressive nationalism. Millions of web pages have sprung up to discuss the book since its release.

In the book, five Chinese grassroots intellectuals asserting China's impending superiority as the world's leader, advocate a hard line against their "enemies," and express dissatisfaction with the West's treatment of China.

The authors denounce Western influences and specifically deride the United States for being "irresponsible, lazy, and greedy, and engaged in robbery and cheating." They blame the United States for causing the current global recession which "reflects an overall corruption of the American society."

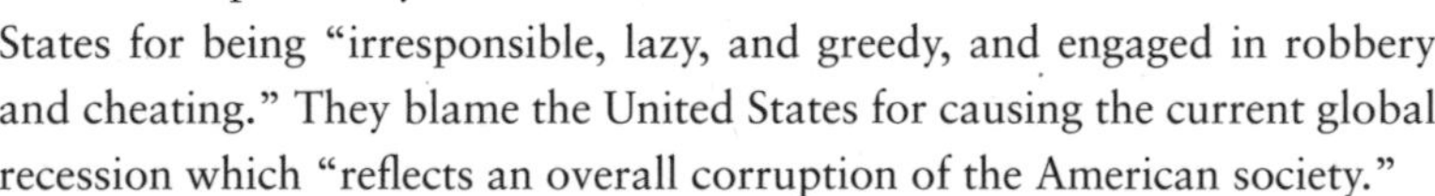

The authors urge the Chinese people to "conduct business with a sword in hand" and advocate more stern foreign policies. "We should incorporate retribution and punishment into our diplomatic strategies." The authors call for the emergence of a group of heroes to "lead our people to successfully control and use more resources, ridding [the world of] of bullies and bringing peace to good people."

Source: Edited from http://www.allgov.com/ViewNews/Unhappy_China_90406 April 2009 and *Shanghai Daily* article, 23 March 2009. The authors, Wang Xiaodong, Liu Yang, Song Qiang, Huang Jisu, and Song Xiaojun, work for at Xinhua, China's government controlled news agency. The book was published shortly before the Copenhagen Global Climate Change Conference which China was widely accused of undermining.

A taste of how this might manifest itself was highlighted in a 2009 bestselling book called *Unhappy China* (see box). The authors portrayed China as a nation with a proud past, which has been tarnished by foreign aggression, greed and wrongful castigation.

How China conducts itself, how it responds to international pressure for cuts in pollution, oil use and water conservation in the coming years, needs to be understood by looking through this prism. China has a strong desire for goods and resources. It prizes wealth as a means to show off its achievements. It also has a strong sense of having been wronged and a belief that it has a "national right" to control the resources that remain.

China's new nationalism runs deep. When America accidentally bombed the Chinese embassy in Belgrade in 1999, 100,000 demonstrators descended on the US embassy in Beijing armed with bricks, stale tomatoes and flaming torches. The state even provided the transport, torches and rotten fruit for hurling. In 2005, when the Japanese Education Ministry approved new school books, which largely ignored its brutal military past, riots broke out in ten Chinese cities. Citizens were notified by SMS that it was their patriotic duty to protest. Similarly, in 2008, there were large-scale anti-French demonstrations in more than twenty cities after the Olympic torch relay in Paris was cut short due to protests over China's policy on Tibet.

A 2009 poem helps further illustrate how far the sense of nationalism and anger towards foreigners has penetrated the psyche of some Chinese school children. It refers to falling Western values, pathetic Europe and the encouragement given to the youngsters to step ruthlessly over wily anti-Chinese forces. Fans can sing along on YouTube.

Go China![6]

Snowstorm, freely falling down to earth, like western values
Despair fills the sky, ice covers the earth
Did China retreat?
No. The Olympics were a success! We are victorious!
Hot blood and iron will of Chinese people, lighten up the dark world like burning the holy flame
The rivers and mountains, ever more colorful and beautiful

Earthquakes, shifting back and forth like the positions
of [French President] Sarkozy, with his dirty tricks, trying
to shake the great China
Did China retreat?
No. The Shenzhou-7 [space rocket] launched. We are
victorious!
Pathetic Europe will never stop the insurmountable force of
our great dynasty
Just the aftershocks from the earthquake would destroy
France!
The happy flowers flourish in the oil fields on Tarim Basin
The suona [musical instrument] sings aloud in the Tawang
district of the Himalayas
Historically accumulated resentment fill the Ryukyu Trench
Smiles in Sun Moon Lake became a miraculous flower in the
Pacific Ocean
Do not waver, do not slow down, do not make big changes
Do not change the flag, do not turn back
Step ruthlessly over all anti-China forces
The giant ship full of patches, raise up the brand new sail
Spirits are high, crash through the waves, the wind is at our
back
Go China!
China the Greatest!

Be Careful What You Wish For

It is easy for those in the West to say that China will need to change when it takes a bigger role on the world stage, and that it will need to calm such sensitivities and adopt the moral framework of enlightened societies when its businesses move abroad.

The Chinese are unlikely to see it that way, however, and the evidence from their recent activities abroad supports this concern.

Most overseas investments by Chinese companies have, so far, been in less-developed countries, notably Africa. In a report[7] on Chinese investments in Africa, including the countries of Angola, Botswana, Ghana, Kenya, Malawi, Namibia, Nigeria, South Africa, Zambia and Zimbabwe, researchers found Chinese companies were "among the worst employers everywhere." It said China's relationship with Africa was that of a "classical colonial exchange," with China exporting raw materials and importing goods. The study said that Chinese companies undercut African companies and push them out of business, bringing few benefits to local economies. "If we complain, they fire us," said one Namibian worker at a construction site in Windhoek, who was being paid $0.55 an hour by his Chinese employer—about half the legal minimum wage for entry-level construction workers.

At the Collum coal mine in Zambia, in 2010, Chinese employers[8] shot and wounded eleven workers who demanded better pay and conditions. The workers had been sent underground without protective clothing, were poorly paid and forced to work in conditions where labor laws were routinely flouted. Other workers were also shot during a previous incident at a mine five years earlier. This time, the Chinese employers slipped the country while out on bail, and the diplomats who guaranteed their bail left too.

In 2007 Chinese employers were arrested in Nigeria for caging workers near an oven in the bakery where they were employed without sufficient water. Namibian workers at a Chinese-run mine in Windhoek[9] were given the option of buying their own safety equipment in 2009 or going without, while other workers were told to mix concrete with their hands.

Employees of these overseas Chinese companies rarely receive contracts. The benefits they are legally entitled to are frequently not paid. They are locked into factories, even during their free time. Women are typically dismissed if they become pregnant. In South Africa, a woman's baby died when she was forced to give birth while locked in a factory. Workers are not paid if they become ill or are injured. In Botswana, local assistants in Chinese shops are expected to work seven days a week, with ten-hour days from Monday to Friday and eight hours a day at the weekend. Public holidays are not recognized and there is no overtime pay. Local newspapers claim[10] that eighteenth-century plantation slaves worked fewer hours.

The arrival of many Chinese workers in Africa has also led to an increase in elephant poaching,[11] while thousands of local workers have been displaced by Chinese immigrants, notably in

Kenya, Angola and Malawi,[12] creating unemployment. China has also been accused of serious environmental damage in much of Africa, especially Mozambique, Southern Sudan, and Equatorial Guinea. Much of the local textile industry, which once existed in parts of the continent, has been destroyed by low-cost Chinese imports.

Such have been the consequences of China's business investment overseas. Chinese companies have barely adapted their habits when they have moved abroad, nor paid much heed to local laws. They have been single-mindedly driven by the pursuit of reward and have retained their traditional business practices.

When the same companies reach the shores of America and Europe in large numbers, there will be a clash. With many developed-world governments facing a prolonged period of low growth and high unemployment, they will desperately need the inward investment that Chinese companies will be offering. The question is: How much will they be willing to compromise on their values to get it?

Playing for Power

There are also concerns about what China's rise will mean at a geopolitical level. Chinese politicians will participate more in important global debates, such as those on climate change, currency exchange rates and human rights. What will that mean?

A clue comes from the way Chinese companies are approaching the global energy game, in how they are planning to secure their future access to the world's oil, gas and uranium reserves.

If they approach the world's big issues with a similar mindset, then the outlook for Western notions of human rights, democratic freedom and justice is not a happy one.

Until a few decades ago there were only a few big players in the world energy game. On one side were the big consumers, the US, Europe and Japan, which use more than two-thirds of the world's energy. On the other side were the big suppliers of oil and gas, Saudi Arabia, Iran, Iraq and Russia. In the nuclear power business, supply was dominated by the big uranium miners in Australia, Canada and Kazakhstan.

In the last twenty years the picture has changed. World energy demand has risen hugely but the share taken by North America, Europe and Japan has fallen, while the proportion taken by developing countries, notably China, has increased rapidly.

The supply side of the game has changed too. Oil extraction has fallen rapidly in the US, the UK and China. Production in the big conventional fields in Russia, Mexico, Kuwait and Saudi Arabia is now declining too, by 4 to 5 percent a year. In contrast, supplies from Nigeria, Angola, Sudan, Libya, Canada and Venezuela have become much more important.

Oil demand is expected to continue to rise faster in developing countries than in developed countries, while supply will become even more complex and expensive. If demand continues to rise at the current pace, the world's oil reserves will be completely exhausted within a few decades (see chapter ten). With economic success so dependent on energy, any country without secure access to oil, gas and uranium risks having less power, in both senses of the word.

This means that after just more than a century, we are approaching the end game of the conventional oil business. Given the stakes, it seems very unlikely that the world's governments will sit down nicely around a table and come to a gentlemanly agreement to divide up the world's remaining conventional energy supplies, according to some equation based on need. Because energy is vital to each nation's economic and social development we risk a feeding frenzy by the world's governments and their agents over the remaining energy carcass. If the game is played badly, if we squander what is left or fail to find a harmonious compromise, we risk conflict.

China has already grasped the nature of this problem.

The country has two main sources of oil and natural gas. It can access pipelines from Russia and Central Asia, or it can ship fuel from the Middle East, Southeast Asia, Africa or South America. Strategically, the more vulnerable route is across the seas. In the event of war—perhaps a war over resources—the passage of ships from Africa and the Middle East can be blocked very easily. The journey passes through the narrow Straits of Malacca. Any rival wanting to control China or North Asia only needs to cut off this shipping lane to prevent the flow of fuel.

China developed contingency plans more than a decade ago to protect its shipping fleet and the supply of critical resources from this risk. These involve the establishment of a series of ports for communication and defense along the supply route from Africa and the Middle East. Stretching from Lamu in Kenya, and Port Sudan to Hong Kong, the US Department of Defense calls these ports China's "String of Pearls."

The Chinese government also began building land-based pipelines to move fuel supplied from Africa and the Middle East directly from the coast of Myanmar to China. This removes the need for its ships to pass through the Malacca Straits.

Establishing these ports has not been easy and illustrates the lengths to which China will go to secure its fuel and other resources. Like America and Europe before, China has already shown that it can be ruthless. Neither human rights nor democratic institutions need be respected if that is what it takes.

Between Africa or the Middle East and Hong Kong there were few places that China could obviously befriend. Forming a comfortable relationship with the government of the largest country on the route, India, was impossible. India is too much of a rival for the world's future energy resources.

So China established close relationships with countries that would normally be of little interest to Beijing. Many were under the control of governments regarded as brutal or corrupt. These include the governments of India's long-time rivals and neighbors in Pakistan, Sri Lanka and Bangladesh, as well as the military junta in Myanmar.

China has agreements to build ports in Gwadar in Pakistan, at Chittagong in Bangladesh and in Sittwe on Myanmar's coast. An oil terminal is being constructed in Myanmar with a 480-mile pipeline, which will run across the country and connect to China's Yunnan Province. Construction of a natural gas pipeline from Myanmar to southern China will begin in 2012.

The island of Sri Lanka, off the bottom tip of India, has become a key hub.

For more than twenty years Sri Lanka battled a civil war. Insurgents in the north, the Tamil Tiger separatists, were trying to establish an independent state. Despite three attempts at peace

Figure 8.1 China's String of Pearls

Source: *US Department of Defense.*

negotiations there had been years of struggle, which brought both sides to a stalemate.

To establish a port, China needed stability. So it provided funds to the Sri Lankan government, enabling it to bring an end to the war. International funding to the Tigers was also strangled. In just a few weeks in 2009, the Colombo government brought overwhelming force to bear and defeated the insurgents, ending twenty-six years of conflict. Thousands of people died, many of them innocent civilians.

Within months China announced plans to establish a huge port at Hambantota, which may also become a military base. Beijing quickly became Sri Lanka's biggest source of foreign funding, providing \$1.2 billion in 2009. As well as the port, it has announced plans to build a power plant and an arts center in the capital. A new airport is planned and the country's railways are to be upgraded.

The rapid change in the destiny of Sri Lanka has been at a cost, however, both for the island's twenty million inhabitants and the rest of the world.

Justice has been undermined: Beijing helped thwart calls for an independent UN investigation into the Sri Lankan army's tactics and alleged human rights abuses during its final battles against the Tigers.

Democracy has been undermined too. The Sri Lankan president, and one-time film actor Mahinda Rajapaksa and his family have taken almost complete control of the government, with songs lauding him as a king. With the main opposition leader in detention, Rajapaksa handed control of several ministries to his brothers, while another was made Speaker of the Parliament, making it almost impossible for the president to be impeached. The constitution has also been changed so that Rajapaksa can rule for life.

There have also been financial changes. A country that was once under the guiding hand of the International Monetary Fund (IMF) is now able to get along without any further international financial support, despite rising public debt.

These changes were not an objective of Chinese investment. They are a consequence. What has happened politically in Sri Lanka is of little interest to Beijing. All China wanted was stability and a port. Yet Sri Lanka has become beholden to China, although not in any ideological sense. It has also become much less democratic and less just as a result of China's involvement.

China's influence has been growing steadily in many of the world's trouble spots. By providing financial aid and ignoring political or economic repression, Chinese interests in Zimbabwe, Somalia, Sudan and Niger have given renewed legitimacy to questionable regimes. Instead of a greater sense of openness, which the citizens of these countries might have once hoped for, political and social repression is again ignored—or even encouraged—if it brings easier access to resources, just as it was during the West's colonial years.

In Zimbabwe, President Robert Mugabe's opposition rival, Morgan Tsvangirai, believes that his country has mortgaged itself to China. There has even been a crackdown on domestic businesses by their own government because the Chinese demanded that local businessmen stop selling second-hand goods that undercut the price of imports.

Countries like Sudan, Angola, Libya, Congo, Somalia and Iran, where the West has had difficult relations for decades, have become Beijing's close friends. The China National Petroleum Corporation (CNPC) has become the largest shareholder in the Greater Nile Petroleum Operating Company, which controls Sudan's oil fields. Chinese loans and construction companies have also helped rebuild Angola's dams, bridges and railway lines, allowing the country to recover from a long civil war. Funding and help have also been given to build schools, roads, hospitals and a fiber-optic network. As a result, Angola has become China's third biggest source of crude oil. Other big Chinese investments have been made to secure oil from Chad, Gabon and Equatorial Guinea. In 2009, more than one-quarter of China's oil imports came from Africa, with a further 15 percent from Iran.

In Niger, the fight is over uranium. For years, the country's former French colonial masters were the largest buyers of Niger's uranium, which accounted for more than 70 percent of Niger's exports. France's Areva, the world's biggest uranium miner, had a *de facto* monopoly.

Not any longer. Niger awarded its first uranium contract to China in 2009. China offered a better price and infrastructure investment. It also signed a contract to provide an oil refinery, something the Nigerien government had repeatedly asked for but which the big Western oil companies had refused. Beijing even showered "signature" bonuses on those it negotiated with as a reward; and the country's capital, Naimey, got a new zoo.

As in Sri Lanka, though, China's investment brought a change in political power. Within months of the deal being signed there was a *coup d'etat* with a military junta seizing power. Much of the money China had given in bonuses was used by the new government to acquire arms to suppress rival tribes. The price France paid for its uranium rose by 50 percent.

Since then both the French and Chinese have announced additional investments. France will open a new uranium mine in 2013, which will make the country the world's biggest supplier after Kazakhstan. China has promised new pipelines and a coal-fired power station.

As in Sri Lanka and Zimbabwe, however, it is doubtful that many of Niger's people will see very much of the country's new wealth. They will have even less say in their country's development. Power has been consolidated in the hands of a few and there are no signs that these new riches will be used for the greater good.

Such practices and consequences are likely to become more common. As the great powers fight for world's resources, there is a risk that the rule of law will be further set aside by all of them. On the other side, the corrupt political leaders of the supplying countries will enrich themselves even more at the expense of their people's and their country's resources. Education, progress and social development will become servants to investment, extraction and control.

Of course, the methods adopted by the Chinese to win access to these resources are well-established. The West used them too, decades ago. America, Europe and Japan are just as guilty of offering poor countries comprehensive and exploitative trade deals combined with aid in return for resources or land. The West has also shown itself to be quite happy to support nasty regimes when it chooses.

In many ways, the Chinese are actually more straight forward about their activities. China does not send in its secret service to manipulate the fate of the leadership in countries where it invests, or to engineer "regime change" like some Western countries might. Unlike some Western agencies, China is not setting out with a plan to undermine democratic institutions or overturn human rights in these places. Or at least there is no indication that this is a specific objective. These outcomes are simple consequences.

Even so, there are two important differences. First, there is much more at stake. During the colonial era, there were enough resources for everyone; today, there are looming shortages. Second, the Chinese are much less constrained by opinion. Those in power are not answerable to any executive. There is no opposition calling for restraint. There are no Chinese non-government organizations (NGOs) lobbying for a more enlightened approach. Instead, Chinese public opinion is silent. Newspapers do not publish leader columns arguing for another approach.

It is not that China and the Chinese people are trying to force these countries backwards, encouraging greater inequality and less freedom, to access oil, gas and uranium. It is simply that almost no one in China cares. If the leadership of a country where Chinese companies want to invest is corrupt, so be it. Beijing does not worry about where the money goes or what is done with it. It does not care if it is used to the detriment of society or to murder those in opposition. All China wants is access to resources as well as business opportunities, and the chance for its construction companies to build new roads, hospitals and bridges. It seeks raw materials and a chance to profit.

On both counts the concern for humanity is the same—that China's investment heralds the start of a new race to the bottom in these countries, morally, economically and environmentally.

An optimist might suggest that China's approach is better. It does not interfere. By making investments in infrastructure, there is a better chance that countries like Angola, Congo and Sudan will industrialize, that they may be able to take concrete steps, literally, towards their own development.

Yet industrialization needs more than new roads, bridges and some hospitals. Education needs more than schools.

In many African countries where China is investing, a prerequisite for industrialization is an end to tribal conflict. Industrialization needs a sustainable and developed agricultural sector to produce food for domestic consumption. It requires a national education policy, manufacturing capabilities and technology. Industrialization does not need democracy, as China itself has shown, but it needs political will. It needs more than an economy based on the extraction of resources for export, funded by another government. It needs more than a political elite taking the proceeds for themselves.

Moreover, industrialization needs jobs and those do not come from China's infrastructure investments. From India, where China is building power stations, to the port of Sri Lanka and the oil refinery in Niger, China brings its own workforce for every job.

With the stakes so high there is an increased risk that the opposite will occur. That instead of these countries being given the chance to develop, human rights abuses, political cronyism and environmental degradation will proliferate. There is a risk that those seeking access to the resources will care little about the development of these countries or their peoples. All the investors want is stability so that they can get to the resources easily, which is more likely with a dictatorship than a democracy. Africa and many other parts of the world risk becoming resources' battlefields, with their peoples the biggest losers.

At the beginning of the twenty-first century the peoples of much of Africa, Pakistan, Bangladesh, Sri Lanka and Myanmar might have hoped that they would soon be able to industrialize. They might have thought their time had come. Their citizens might reasonably have anticipated the dawn of pluralistic societies. They might have expected that economic growth would bring democratic governments, meritocratic work practices, a better distribution of wealth, decent healthcare, a proper education system and the chance of social enlightenment. After centuries of exploitation, the peoples of these countries might have hoped they could achieve something close to developed-country standards in the coming decades. With their vast natural and human resources, such hopes were not unrealistic.

Yet it seems unlikely that they will get what they hoped for, despite holding so many advantages and so many of the world's natural resources. More probably, they will remain small tokens in a much grander game. They may get some roads, railways and hospitals that they did not have before. And the occasional zoo.

But within a few decades, they will have lost everything they would have needed to fuel their own development. When they need oil, or gas, or uranium to fuel their own growth it will be gone. Instead of becoming democracies, their peoples will remain under the control of autocratic regimes. They will be bled dry by China and the West. Then they will be left to drift.

There will be no enlightenment here.

Endnotes

1. Chinese culture dominates China, Taiwan, Hong Kong and Singapore. Because localized ethnic-Chinese have built great financial power, it is also strong in Thailand, Malaysia, Indonesia and Vietnam.
2. "China: Spirituality or Materialism," Arthur Rosenfeld, *Huffington Post*, November 9, 2009, with permission.
3. Kroll Annual Global Fraud Survey, *Financial Times,* UK, October 18, 2010.
4. "China jails teachers and parents for hi-tech exam cheating," Tania Branigan. http://www.guardian.co.uk/world/2009/apr/03/china-jails-exam-cheats.
5. "National Humiliation, History Education, and the Politics of Historical Memory," Zheng Wang, *International Studies Quarterly* (2008) 52, 783–806.
6. Video performance: "2009 Go China!" Translated by Bob Chen. http://chinadigitaltimes.net/2008/12/video-performance-2009-go-china/.
7. "Chinese Investments in Africa: A Labour Perspective," The African Labour Research Network, July 2009.
8. "Zambia accused of ignoring Chinese abuse of mine workers." *Financial Times*, UK, October 20, 2010.
9. "Chinese bad employers in Africa," Erin Conway-Smith, *Global Post* (Boston), July 29, 2009. http://www.globalpost.com/dispatch/africa/090727/chinese-bad-employers-africa.
10. "Shop Assistants in Chinese Stores Maltreated?," Edward Bule, November 13, 2009, allafrica.com.
11. "Chinese influx in Africa rekindles elephant poaching," Reuters report published on August 31, 2009 by RNW Radio Netherlands Worldwide.
12. "Africa's Poor Don't See China as a Great Power," *Asia Sentinel Report*, November 20, 2009.

Part 3

The Implications of These Failures Will be Hard

Part one looked at how modern economics has failed us. It showed how the rise of individualism and an unrestrained free-market philosophy have led to a failed financial system. It looked at how we are under-pricing the world's resources and wasting them as a result. It discussed the rise of inequality and greed. And, although most of the financial problems are most obvious in the West, it showed that weak economic thinking around the world is causing asset bubbles, wrongly priced products and a foolish belief that human progress should be dependent on rising consumer spending.

The second part looked at how poorly equipped we are to deal with these problems. Standards of innovation and education are declining in much of the world. Many of our societies have become superficial, with a loss of social purpose. It discussed how politicians, faced with no binding social ideology to empower them, have resorted to the use of fear to control us. They have privatized snooping and reduced our freedom, passing too much power onto private firms seeking profit instead of social development. It also discussed how the rise of China will accelerate many of these trends, although not by deliberate design. China's approach to democracy, human and workers' rights as well as its views on the exploitation of the world's resources will become more prevalent in the years to come, and will risk making existing global problems even worse.

Part three looks at what happens next. It looks at the future we face if humankind does not get off the current path. It looks at the long-term implications of the financial crisis, at the way resource shortages will force us to change our way of life, about how standards of health will decline and pressures for conflict will rise. Without radical change, the future for much of humanity is raw and cold.

Part four looks at the options, about how we can respond to the challenges ahead, about how we can avoid making the situation worse and what we can do to stop at least some of these problems recurring.

9

WE WILL BECOME FINANCIALLY POORER

The world owes more than the world can pay.

Ralph Waldo Emerson

Massive financial challenges with unpredictable but deeply damaging consequences lie ahead of us. Most Western societies are broke. Consumer borrowing is too high, bank debt is too great, and many governments have borrowed too much. The West and Japan will need to rebuild their financial foundations.

One of the most obvious effects of this rebuilding is that spending will have to fall. Consumer spending, that precious pillar of modern economics, has to shrink.

To return to balance, most developed-world consumers will need to cut back, repay what they owe, and live within their means. Similarly, banks will have to stop lending and put their accounts in order. That will take time. Governments will have to reduce their spending too, slashing their budgets for everything from welfare to defense and education. They will need to lay off tens of thousands of employees, accelerating the spiral of decline.

If spending is not cut, millions of people, hundreds of banks and at least a dozen of the world's biggest governments face bankruptcy and financial ruin.

So our future will be one of three financial worlds. As well as the developed world and the developing world, there will be the undeveloping world—the countries that will shift backwards, economically and socially, as the cutbacks take effect.

These changes will have profound consequences. The fallout will last for years, perhaps decades. In the US and much of Europe, the debts, as well as the pension and healthcare liabilities, will bring stagnation, higher taxation and misery. China will face a slowdown, with rising inflation and the risk of instability. In Japan, bankruptcy looms in the shadows ahead.

Even then, the reductions in spending may not work. The debts are so great and the effects of the changes so unpredictable that even years of hardship could result in a financial implosion. There is no guarantee of success.

But Answers Are Easy, Aren't They?

Some economists still claim that there are easy solutions to the weighty economic and financial problems we face, that the gloomy predictions are naught but scaremongering. They see simple answers to the debt burden that will make taking any nasty medicine unnecessary.

Economists from the Western financial press chant the steps we need to take, like a mantra: the world needs China to let its currency appreciate; the US needs to boost exports; we need Chinese and German consumers to go out and spend, because they save too much; the economies of South Korea and Japan need reform to make them more open; and the European Union (EU) needs to liberalize regulations and cut back on welfare.

This is the road to salvation, we are told.

Yet this is nonsense. China's currency is its own business, and tweaking currencies will not take away trillions of dollars of Western debt. Nor can the US suddenly boost its exports. America would need something to export, something that all the world wants in unheard of quantities, to correct its imbalances. And it would need to be uniquely competitive in whatever it is. Simply saying that the US needs to grow overseas shipments does not make it possible.

Cajoling the Chinese and Germans to spend more is also daft. More than 60 percent of the German economy is already consumption based, only slightly less than in the US. So there is not much scope for growth there. And although there is more opportunity for higher spending in China, the Chinese like to save—and for good reason. One of the main causes of the Western financial mess is that the Americans, British, Australians, Irish and peoples of many other countries simply spent and borrowed too much. Encouraging the Germans and the Chinese to do the same is not a solution. That will only worsen the problem.

Similarly, the governments and peoples of South Korea, Japan and Europe have resisted reforms to open up their economies and liberalize their welfare systems, not because they do not understand what they are being asked to do, but because they choose not to. It is not their way. It does not fit with their economic and social systems. Just because America and some other countries in the West think it is a good idea does not make it so. The citizens of these countries believe that such ideas and the free-market system have not worked. The South Koreans, the Japanese and the Europeans, with their restrictive labor practices and unsustainable welfare systems, have made a choice. This is the way they want to do things. It is not the American way, it is not the free-market way, but that does not make it wrong.

The Long Tail

Rather than looking to simple solutions, the West has to accept reality. It is facing a prolonged period of economic decline. It needs to learn to reduce its debts and live within its means.

Financial bubbles are not like balloons that are quickly blown up and instantly deflated. A bubble is more like a gigantic bathtub, the size of a house. It fills ever faster until it suddenly overflows. Only then do we realize the scale of the problem. So we take out the plug. But the hole is so small, and the volume of water is so great, that the tub will take years to empty.

The effects of the Great Crash in 1929 endured for decades. Although the stock-market bubble grew and deflated comparatively quickly, the consequences lasted much longer. Similarly, the bursting of the stock-market bubble in 1989 in Japan has had an impact that has run for years.

Before 1921, stock prices in the US had been stagnant for more than twenty years. But during the following eight years they rose, slowly at first, and then very rapidly. Newspapers at the time talked of a new age of scientific glory, progress and wealth and there was soon an irrational belief that share prices would continue rising forever. At the peak, the market was more than 500 percent higher than its low point.

In six days shares lost 30 percent of their value. Then there was a recovery which lasted several months. Bullish shareholders fooled themselves into thinking the value of their stocks would recover. Despite the irrational growth over the previous eight years and the warning sign they had been given, they believed, just as more recent investors believed during the technology bubble in the late 1990s in America, there was a new "paradigm" that would prevail.

Eventually, of course, the market collapsed. Panic took hold and the index, which had peaked in 1929 at 381 points, eventually fell to a low of just 41.

The decline, however, did not happen over a few weeks or months. Markets and economies can fall fast but they rarely drop like stones for very long. It took almost three years to reach the bottom, in July 1932. And, although there was a recovery after that, the market did not bounce back quickly. It took until 1954 before the Dow reached 300 points again—the full impact of the crash lasted more than a quarter of a century. In 1929 the US had a GDP of $103 billion. By 1933 this had fallen by almost half—to $56 billion—and it took until 1941 before 1929 levels returned. In real terms, if you take into account inflation, it took nearly twice as long.

The pattern was almost identical in Japan in the 1980s. After many years of stagnating stock prices, the Tokyo stock market began to rise. For five or six years there was only slow growth. Then there was a phase of rapid expansion. By 1989 the Nikkei was 500 percent higher than at the beginning of its growth cycle a few years earlier.

What followed was almost identical too. After peaking, the value of shares dropped a little before bouncing back for a while. Then there was a much steeper crash followed by more than twenty years of decline. The market and economy have still not recovered. Having peaked at 38,916 points in December 1989, the Nikkei 225 Index stood at just 7,500 in 2009, a decline of more than 80 percent. For more than twenty-six consecutive years Japan saw no net gain in stock prices.

So big economic crashes lead to big hangovers, which can last a very long time. They herald a period of stagnation, a bear market, which usually lasts for decades. In the US, the *shortest* bear market of the twentieth century lasted seventeen years. Big bubbles change lives.

Unfortunately, the 2007 bubble was larger than both the 1929 bubble in the US and the bubble in Japan in 1989. When it finally bursts, the effects will be just as prolonged.

All Comes Tumbling Down

One prediction that can be made with some certainty is that the value of stocks and shares will fall much further in the next five to ten years. Given the size of the bubble, it is clear that the 2007 correction was not the big one; it was just an early warning bell. The main crash is still to come. Even at the start of 2011, most stock prices remained well above their fundamental worth, based on the economic outlook.

It is not just that there is an overdue correction on the way. It is that the debt hangover will force cutbacks, which will reduce consumption and economic growth, for years to come. The engine will go into reverse, forcing share prices to fall. There will be an extended period of economic decline, with lower sales volumes for many businesses and so lower returns. Capacity utilization will fall, increasing the average cost of many products too.

Consumption has to decline because Western consumers need to save more. They will not be able to borrow as before because of the weakness of many banks. Governments will also have to put up taxes to try and repay their debts. This will cut the spending power of most citizens even further. Baby boomers will need to replenish their depleted retirement funds too, and so they will have to save more and spend less. Food and fuel price inflation, caused by water and other resource shortages, will also affect the ability of consumers to spend. More money will be spent on soap, carrots and shampoo, leaving less for iPads, new washing machines and cigarettes. Western consumers will need to make more compromises, choosing what they need over what they might want.

Because of this, the sales and value of most large companies will decline in Europe and the US, although some will see steeper drops than others. Demand for discretionary consumer goods will see the biggest declines. Sales of electronics goods, holidays and cars will fall to a level far below their peak volume and stay there. Demand should remain strong for essential items, such as foodstuffs, pharmaceuticals and energy. Even here, though, the profits of companies in these businesses will be squeezed as Western consumers tighten their belts. The mix of products that consumers buy will also change. Instead of pre-prepared meals and *foie gras*, shoppers will want more pasta, minced meat and bread.

These changes will be reflected in the Western world's stock markets. The share prices of car makers, washing machine manufacturers and ready-made meal producers, which are overly dependent on European and US markets, will fall sharply. The stock prices of companies supplying more essential products and services in these markets will be stronger, although they will decline too, because of the overall drop in economic activity to come.

Some businesses may rise in value—notably those that may be of interest to Chinese and Indian companies seeking acquisitions. These are likely to be in the engineering and technology sectors, as well as some retailing businesses where Asian companies may want to establish distribution networks in developed markets.

Because there will be more sellers than buyers, and because real incomes will stagnate or decline, the value of most other established assets in the West will fall, from houses to yachts and second-hand cars. But in an "age of austerity" the value of second-hand clothing, computers and other items that can be reused should rise.

In some parts of Europe, house prices will return to the levels of the early 1990s in real terms and, in some cases, in nominal terms too. In early 2011 they remained vastly over-priced as a percentage of average incomes in many countries.

Even thereafter, without any upward economic momentum, there will be more downward than upward price pressure. For those people who have large homes in the countryside, which require a car and are better suited to a large family, the prospects are especially bleak. In almost every developed country, demographic changes will mean there will be fewer buyers for these sorts of houses in the next twenty years. With oil prices likely to rise too, having a house that is expensive to get to, as well as to heat and maintain, will become progressively less affordable. This will be reflected in the price.

With the stagnation in real incomes, a fall in spending and drop in asset values to come, many Western banks will find that their balance sheets get progressively weaker. The value of most of the assets they have lent against will continue to fall. For some banks this will spell disaster. Some will face bankruptcy. But most will probably adopt the same strategy as banks did in Japan after 1989. They will continue to show the value of the loans on their books at inflated levels—because to show them in any other way would push them over the edge.

As a result, the West will see a gradual rise in the number of comatose banks—banks that are neither dead nor alive. They may not close their doors but they will not lend either. This will also limit the opportunities for any sustained recovery in the West. As in Japan in the 1990s, these banks will have to be carefully managed for years in the hope that asset values will eventually rise and they can recover.

Goodbye Stimulus Packages, Hello Savage State Cutbacks

It is tempting to hope that these banks will be bailed out by Western governments again, although this is very unlikely. The governments of the US and Europe cannot keep bailing out their failed banks. Just as in Japan in the 1990s, Western governments know that to do so will lead to their own financial collapse. Few can take on any more debt. If they do, they face debt downgrades, default and currency collapse. Nor can these governments close their struggling banks; they support the fate of so many people and companies. Millions of people have taken out mortgages with these banks, which they cannot refinance or repay quickly. Thousands of businesses are similarly stuck, with loans they cannot refinance. Closing the banks would reveal these otherwise hidden troubles. So the Japanese strategy, and the creation of un-dead banks, is probably the only way open to most Western countries in the years ahead.

These prognostications are certainly gloomy. Yet, given the scale of the debt overhang, they probably represent the best financial outlook that can be expected for many Western countries. Even then, they may not save some nations from something worse.

In the US and many parts of Europe, notably the UK, Greece, Portugal, Spain, Iceland, Ireland and possibly Italy, there is a danger that no amount of belt-tightening will be able to stave off a national default. There could still come a time when the debts of many of these countries will need to be rescheduled. Those that lent to them will have to take a "haircut" as the bankers say; they will have to accept a loss on their investments. The sovereign wealth funds, banks, pension funds and others who lent to these countries, who bought their bonds in the belief that they were safe, will lose much of what they invested. Horrific as that might seem, it would not be the first time it has happened.

Such rescheduling, or defaulting, will not be easy, however, even if it becomes progressively more tempting. The governments that take this course would see the value of their currencies fall and their borrowing costs rise steeply. Interest rates would need to rise too. This would result in yet higher costs for those people already struggling with mortgages and loans they cannot pay, along with a further fall in house prices. It would also increase the rate of inflation, partly because many of these countries import so much of what they consume.

For those countries inside the eurozone, the consequences are especially hard to guess. Many speculate that Spain, Ireland, Greece, and others, may have to leave the single-currency zone. Yet this it very unlikely and would be enormously complex to manage because there is no mechanism for it to happen. Relaunching their old currencies would also risk bankruptcy because they would quickly fall in value while their debts would remain in euros. Yet staying within the eurozone will become more difficult too, not least because the troubles of weak European countries would drag down the bloc's stronger northern economies, notably Germany and France. Such tensions risk unleashing unpredictable forces, which will test the resolve of the entire European Union to stay united, unless they are carefully managed. There would either need to be some sort of fiscal integration of members, so that the weaker countries would be made to pay for their own profligacy, or there would be a risk that the stronger countries will leave, unraveling sixty years of history.

During the coming years there will also be a great shift in the relative strength of currencies and, with that, a shift in economic power. If current trends continue, the economic and political domination so long enjoyed by the US will gradually come to an end. America's belief in the free-market model, in its superior technology and science, is now viewed differently by other nations, notably those in Asia and in much of continental Europe. America was acting like a monopoly power, pushing a philosophy that did not work. Together with its allies, the US faces a future where the high ground has been lost. The US will remain the world's biggest military and economic power for another two decades or so. But its influence will wane. It can accept this change and take the difficult consequences that will follow or resist it, although it may then risk even more.

Even today, despite being burdened by debt and an economic model that no longer works, the US and its allies still think that they control the world's economic events. Yet the financial shake up of 2007 and the debt hangover have not just been financially damaging, they have also undermined the West's influence. Developing countries may have disliked America's imperialistic behavior but they were cowed by its power and wealth. Not any longer.

So the mighty US dollar is in the firing line too. It remains the world's biggest reserve currency, accounting for about 70 percent of funds held. But the value of the dollar is not a fair reflection of the future strength of the US economy. The US dollar needs to fall in value, to reflect the weakness of the US outlook and the levels of debt America carries.

This change will take time, partly because it will result in a dramatic loss of American financial power and economic strength.

Gradually though, as the depth of America's problems become clear, the pressure to find an alternative reserve currency will grow. As the dollar drops in value, countries supplying commodities as well as those with large quantities of dollar-denominated savings will find a more reliable alternative. This may be the euro, or even the Chinese yuan if it becomes freely convertible one day.

More likely perhaps is that the world will look towards using a basket of currencies. Some Middle-Eastern countries have already suggested that oil needs to be priced this way. This would free traders as well as buyers and sellers from tying their future to a declining currency. Creating an international currency for oil and other commodities would also have the advantage of more stable prices. Such plans remain embryonic, but are likely to gain more favor as America's economy struggles and its debts worsen.

More Air Will Not Work

In trying to combat so many financial problems and eradicate the accumulated Western debts, some economists have suggested that a dose of inflation would be a good thing. If prices rise, the thinking goes, the debts will become smaller. Owing $10,000 when you have an income of $5,000 becomes less of a burden when inflation brings a pay rise. The debt stays the same but the ability to pay it off improves.

Certainly, inflation will rise in the West and many other countries in the coming years, with much higher food and energy prices. Countries that reschedule their debts will experience even higher inflation, as their costs of borrowing grow and their currencies drop in value.

Yet the notion that inflation will gradually eradicate the debt is wrong, according to the IMF. Inflation would further reduce the value of a country's currency, meaning imported goods become more expensive. Even if wages double, the cost of much of what they are used for would rise too, reducing the benefit. Inflation also puts up interest rates, which makes the burden of servicing the debts greater. Moreover, government spending, especially for welfare and healthcare, has to rise too, as wages grow. To finance this, governments would need to borrow more, making their country's debts even worse. For the US government in particular, stoking deliberate inflation makes even less sense. Many of the bonds it has issued are inflation-protected. If inflation rises, so do the costs of debt.

According to the IMF, inflation would reduce the growth in US debt-to-GDP by less than a quarter. So the bulk of the debt would remain. The only practical way out of a consumer debt trap is for people to spend less and save more. The alternative is bankruptcy. For governments, excess debt means tax hikes and spending cuts. The alternative for them is to default and face the ensuing chaos. Either way, the outcome will be the same—decades of low growth and economic stagnation.

There are no easy options.

You Need Another Hole in That Belt

The prolonged period of belt tightening that is needed will be made harder by a continuing decline in asset prices, especially in Europe where householders cannot walk away from their mortgages as they can in the US. Their loans will effectively get bigger while their real incomes fall, accelerating the spiral of decline.

For those wanting to sell their houses or any other assets, such as stocks, shares, cars or yachts, there will be the added problem of a diminishing number of buyers. Unless the assets can be sold to those with rising incomes, such as the Chinese, sellers will struggle to find a buyer willing to pay the price they want. This applies to both private and public assets. Pension and investment funds will have particular problems, with more and more people wanting to draw down their savings but fewer and fewer people willing to buy the investments of these companies.

A further risk of the belt tightening is what it will mean socially. Even in 2009, after two years of government stimulus, one in seven Americans was living in poverty.[1] This was the highest number in the fifty-one years since the US Census Bureau started measuring poverty rates. That number is expected to grow.

As governments and companies cut back and as consumption declines, shifting away from the frivolous to the essential, unemployment will rise steadily. Those with jobs face lower wages. Not only will this worsen the financial situation of millions, forcing them into great hardship, but the rise in unemployment will become, at least in most of Europe, an additional welfare problem. Governments will need to simultaneously cut spending and find more money to support those in need. The choices they face will be harsh. Do they cut welfare payments or reduce spending elsewhere: In defense, education, healthcare or infrastructure?

With the rise in nationalist and protectionist sentiments already apparent in many parts of the world since 2007, partly through the increasing influence of right-wing political groups, the risk of social instability will grow too. In tough times there is a natural desire to protect what is seen as traditional and local. People seen as job-stealing and welfare-cheating risk being expelled from their adoptive countries, even though this may make little economic sense and will only raise nationalistic sentiments further.

The power of trade unions will grow too. Strikes, closures, sit-ins and street demonstrations will see a resurgence, although there is probably little these can achieve. A period of prolonged industrial action does nothing to cut a nation's debts. It may even make them worse, by reducing investment and undermining confidence. Such worries may not put people off, however, especially where there is a strong sense of anger and injustice. In some places, these strikes will inevitably turn nasty. There is even a risk of social order breaking down, especially in countries where spending cuts have reduced police and military strength.

Extreme political parties are likely to re-emerge, adding more spice to an already bitter soup. As the economic pain grows, nationalists and communists will find it easy to grow like weeds through today's weakly nourished political soil. The sense of wrong that many Western citizens will feel, and their valid belief that their suffering is down to the greed of a few, will easily attune them to radical politics. The dumbing-down of society means that those wanting to foment such angry sentiments won't have to do much work.

While the West struggles, Asia and many other developing regions will find progress less easy than before. China, India and much of South America will have to become more independent. They will face rising inflation, lower growth and rumbling discontent as a result. Their citizens will feel aggrieved. They will feel cheated because their promised journey to riches has been delayed. When they realize it is likely to be canceled completely, they will feel angrier still. Additional manufacturing jobs in Germany and other parts of the world will be lost, while China and other developing nations try to gain jobs and maintain their pace of economic progress—unless some form of protectionism is introduced. Yet this too would probably make the whole situation worse, by cutting global trade and raising international tensions.

For Japan, which has already experienced more than twenty years of stagnation and decline, economic collapse beckons. It is impossible to say when, although the rebuilding costs after the 2011 earthquake and tsunami are likely to hasten the day, given the additional borrowing that will be needed for rebuilding. As with many countries in Europe, the debts are just too big for Japan to survive without some sort of crisis. Although Japanese citizens are still comparatively wealthy, and many Japanese corporations are strong, the government has borrowed more than it can repay. At some point a crunch will come and the stoicism of the Japanese will be tested even further. The only real option will be to write-off the debts and start again with a new currency. All those savings risk being lost in the process.

In the next chapter, we will explore one factor that may reverse the increasing number of job losses in the West. With a growing shortage of energy, higher transportation costs may make it less viable to make goods in one part of the world and ship to another. An energy crisis could bring a resurgence of local economic activity.

Yet while this may offer a partial solution to some the world's financial problems, it would not come without its own difficult implications.

Endnote

1. US Census Bureau report "Income, Poverty and Health Insurance Coverage in the United States," 2009.

10

OUR WAY OF LIFE WILL CHANGE

It is not necessary to change. Survival is not mandatory.

William Edwards Deming, US Statistician

The financial woes are tough, but they do not affect everyone and they are not evenly spread across the world. The most badly affected countries are in the West, particularly the US and much of Europe. Other places such as Australia, South Korea and Japan are also over-burdened with debt, although in different ways. In Australia and South Korea the problem is consumer debt, in Japan it is government debt. But countries like China and much of the rest of Asia are largely unaffected. They will suffer from the implications of the West's profligacy, but they have savings to cushion the effects. Moreover, the world's financial problems can be solved. It may take years, and it may bring waves of poverty and hardship to millions, but humankind can survive the financial crisis.

The same cannot be said for the world's resource shortages. The resource challenges affect us all and there are no easy solutions to some of the difficulties that lie ahead. We do not have enough water and cannot make more, or at least not practically. Nor can we replace the world's oil, copper, uranium and coal reserves when they have been used up. We cannot refill the oceans with fish, coral and mammals when they have gone. We cannot regenerate the rainforests when they have become deserts, drained of all their nutrients.

The outlook for many of our natural and mineral resources, including the world's fresh water supplies, forests and other species, is bleak. But it is the shortage of oil that will first force us to change the way those of us in the developed world live.

In the Energy Battles, No One Will Play Nicely

While water shortages affect billions of us, the challenges we face concerning the lack of oil will affect almost everyone. And, unlike the water shortages, which will mostly impact the poor and powerless, at least at first, the oil shortages will hit the wealthiest nations hardest. Unless we can find an alternative—and soon—we face a future where the costs of many items we use in the developed world will rise steadily. Air travel, diesel trains, cars, trucks, container ships, antiseptics, nail polishes, shampoos, perfumes, paints and heart valves all need oil; and developing an alternative for most of these at a comparable cost is likely to be impossible.

Oil is the best source of energy known to humankind and makes our modern lifestyles possible. But we have become addicted to the stuff. If it ran out tomorrow we would be plunged into something resembling the Dark Ages within a week. Most of our land, sea and air transport systems would grind to a halt. The lights would literally go out in many places. We would be without many vital hospital supplies and modern anesthetics. Oil is critical, it is more essential to our lives than we can probably imagine.

Of course it will not happen like this. We will not wake up one day and find that there is no more oil. We know that day will come, but we assume it is in some distant decade, long after most of us have gone. We assume there will be a transition period when we can develop alternatives. We can grow bio-fuels, build more nuclear power plants and learn how to capture power from the sun, wind and waves efficiently. We can develop cars that use batteries or hydrogen. We have the answers already; we just need to develop them further.

The trouble comes in the timing and the cost. There is evidence to suggest that an oil shortage will be with us sooner than most of us realize. The US and German military authorities believe that we will see the early effects of an oil shortage within the next few years—and certainly within the next decade. If they are right, we are worryingly unprepared. To build nuclear power stations takes decades and costs billions. They also bring their own set of concerns. We have no immediate alternative to aviation fuel, gasoline or diesel for transport—which is where most of the oil is used. Replacements that can be produced cost effectively in high volumes are more than a decade away. And even when we have perfected them, what do we do with the 900 million vehicles already on our roads? Or with most of the world's shipping fleet and the thousands of aircraft that use today's oil-derived fuels?

There is another more important component in the transition from conventional fuels to alternatives we often forget. The price. As countries like China and India grow, demand will rise. China is now the world's biggest energy user[1] and its needs will rise in the decades to come. Even if our existing supplies could cope, this would push up prices.

A further problem is the type of oil we have left. Much of what remains is difficult and expensive to extract, so this will push the price up even more.

As well as being the source of so much that drives the wheels of our world, oil is also a curse that threatens it. The geopolitical curse is that oil is concentrated in just a few locations. Like some ingredient that did not blend into the global cake mixture properly, this upsets the balance. It results in massive transfers of wealth from the rich nations to a few, mostly poor ones, and has created global tensions for years.

A world without oil, or even a world with expensive oil, is hard to imagine. Cheap oil has become part of the political, social, and economic lifeblood of most countries. Our suburbs depend on it, as do our food supplies. Our world is organized around its supply and use.

Demand for oil has risen steadily for decades, with a hiccup in the late 1970s. In 2010, world-wide oil consumption reached eighty-five million barrels per day. With each barrel holding forty-two gallons, that means three and one-half billion gallons are consumed every day—half a gallon for each man, woman, and child on earth. The US is the biggest user, consuming 23 percent of the total. China, the second biggest consumer, used two-thirds less. But while demand in the US is falling, it has been rising rapidly in China and many other developing countries.

Thankfully, there is still plenty of oil. The world is full of fossil fuel. So far, we have only consumed just more than half of the oil reserves that we know about. But there is considerable evidence that we have already passed the peak of global oil production. That does not mean the oil has gone. It is more like climbing a mountain. We appear to be over the crest and are now marching down the other side (see Figure 10.1).

At first glance, reaching the peak seems to be of little importance. If it took us more than a century to consume half the oil, there must be sufficient available for years to come. The trouble comes when we look at the rate of growth in demand and the rate of decline in supply. The output from the main oil fields is declining at a rate of 4 to 5 percent a year. We are not finding new oil at anything like the rate needed to make up this shortfall. And countries like China and India, as well as many of those in the Middle East, are using more and more each year.

In 2010, two-thirds of our oil came from about 300 fields,[2] almost all of which have passed their peak. Most were more than fifty years old. Oil production has been in steep decline in the

Figure 10.1 Chart World Peak Oil

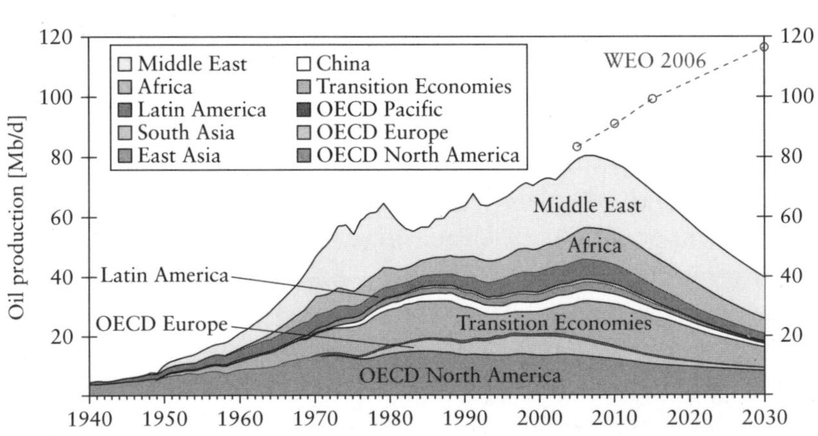

Source: *Energy Watch Group, with permission*

United States, Mexico, China, Norway, Nigeria, Indonesia and Oman, and many other places, for more than a decade. Onshore oil output peaked in the 1970s; shallow-water oil production peaked in the 1980s.

The crux of the problem can be explained with some simple arithmetic. If the net increase in demand for oil is just 7 percent a year (the loss in output added to the growth in demand), then we only have enough oil left on the planet for ten more years.[3] That is, ten years of growth at 7 percent doubles total demand, and so uses up the remaining half of world reserves. If we can use the stuff more efficiently and cut the rate of growth to just 5 percent a year, then we have enough oil left for fourteen years. At just 3 percent annual growth we have enough oil to last until 2033, by which time it will be completely gone. What is left will not last anything like the 100 years we may imagine.

An added problem is that most of the oil we have left is harder to access. Although there are all sorts of charts and tables that show we still have plenty of oil, most fail to explain the difficulty of extracting what remains. The deep sea rigs in the Gulf of Mexico and many other places, some of which have caused huge environmental damage, are there because the oil that is accessible on land or in shallower waters is mostly gone.

Moreover, what is left is lots of sour, heavy oil. The stuff we really need, the light and sweet crude, which is easiest to turn into aviation and transport fuel, is running out fastest. Much of what remains is unconventional oil—heavy oil, oil shale and tar sands. This type of oil is mostly used for asphalt or bunker fuel. It is much harder to refine into transportation fuel and most refineries are unable to process it. This means producing gasoline, diesel and aviation fuel will get progressively more expensive.

According to the late Matthew Simmons,[4] a well-respected industry expert, the global rate of conventional crude-oil flow is likely to fall steadily during the next ten years to about fifty million barrels of oil a day by 2020.[5] If he is right, we face a 41 percent shortfall within a decade—without *any* growth in demand. Because we will also have to use oil that is harder to access and less suitable for our needs, he thinks we face substantial price hikes and a series of mini oil shocks in the years ahead. His forecasts are backed up by many others. According to the International Energy Agency (IEA), we will need to discover the equivalent of three new Saudi Arabias if we are to meet global oil demand in 2030.

There are also skills and infrastructure problems. Much of the existing oil network is old and rusting, especially in Russia. Many of the rigs need replacing. And the business has an aging workforce because there is a lack of engineers and geologists entering the industry.

There is a social problem too. Much of the anticipated growth in demand comes from the Middle East, one of the major sources of supply. To meet their own needs these countries will have to cut their exports by 25 percent by 2020—assuming the *current* rate of production.

Moreover, of the 600 million people who live in the Organization of the Petroleum Exporting Countries (OPEC), the club for many oil exporters, two-thirds live below the poverty line. Not only are these countries being paid too little for their oil, the revenues they receive are not being distributed fairly. This brings two added worries. First, as the populations of these countries grow, there will be a rising level of discontent over such blatant unfairness and the squandering of their national resources. Second, they are likely to start using even greater quantities of the stuff themselves, partly because it is so under-valued.

When You Are in a Hole, Keep Digging

Faced with so many problems, what can we do?

One option is to use more unconventional oil although this will not be easy. Unconventional oil refers to non-traditional fossil energy sources that can be used to produce liquid fuels similar to gasoline and diesel. They include oil shale, oil sands, very heavy oil and coal, as well as natural gas used to make liquids. There are vast amounts of these distributed around the world.

About 85 percent of the very heavy oil is in Venezuela and its development has been delayed mostly because of where it is located. Production requires expensive technology and very large, long-term investments. The national oil companies in Venezuela do not have the technical capability, while the large Western oil companies have been reluctant to invest in a country where the government is seen as unreliable. So there is plenty of work to do if we are to access this sort of oil.

Another potential source is the tar sands, mostly located in Canada. Tar sands are actually bitumen, a solid form of oil. Again, getting the stuff out is very difficult and expensive. The environmental costs are massive. Extracting the oil requires huge open-cast mines and vast amounts of energy and water. Restoring the land afterwards is hard because of the sludge and the high levels of salt in the waste streams. Extraction also produces huge quantities of carbon dioxide.

Another alternative is oil shale, which is also extremely abundant. Almost two-thirds of the world's oil shale reserves are in the US, mostly in Utah, Wyoming, and Colorado. There are also deposits in China, Brazil, Estonia, Morocco, Jordan and a few other places.

Oil shale is a form of hydrocarbon embedded in rock. But it is even more difficult to extract than oil from tar sands. Some of the big oil companies are working on experimental plants in a handful of locations and volume production exists in China, Estonia and a few other places. It is the main source of energy for electric power generation in Estonia. But getting the oil out of the rock is very expensive and technically complex, needing large quantities of water and energy. It is also environmentally horrible, leaving a scarred landscape and high risks of groundwater pollution. Extraction generates high levels of sulfur emissions and other air pollutants too. Many of the reserves also contain high levels of arsenic. In the US, it is even less attractive as an alternative source of conventional oil because of its location in an arid and fragile environmental area.

An alternative, which is similar but viewed more favorably because the resources are still plentiful, is coal liquefaction—extracting oil and petroleum from coal. Coal is easily the most abundant hydrocarbon on earth. This can be cheap too, and uses an extraction process that is well-established. Moreover, the US, China and India have very large coal deposits, making the idea even more attractive. It is also possible to capture some of the pollutants generated during the process, especially the high levels of carbon dioxide.

The downside is environmental degradation. Coal extraction produces lots of waste much of which contains harmful metals like mercury, uranium and arsenic. Water tables often become polluted. The liquefaction process also produces more greenhouse gases than crude oil production.

The main short-term problem, though, is capacity. To replace the oil we use now would need dozens of coal liquefaction plants, which we haven't even started building. Some exist in South Africa, China and several other countries. Others are being built, notably in India. But our global need far outweighs the possible supply, at least in the short term.

Longer term, the problem is the same as with oil. While we have vast reserves of coal in the world, they are finite and they would be consumed more quickly if we had to use them as a substitute for oil.

At *current* rates of production we have enough coal for more than a century. But much of the information we have on coal reserves is imprecise. During the last twenty years, estimates of the world's reserves have fallen by 20 percent as we have learned more about how to measure them. In 2004, Germany, the UK and Botswana actually downgraded what they once thought were their reserves by 99 percent. Poland cut its estimates in half. In China, now the biggest burner of coal, data on their reserves have not been published since 1990. In other places the mines have been accidentally flooded making access all but impossible. So we are not entirely sure how much coal we really have. But we know we are using it up quickly. America, which is the world's second largest coal producer, saw its coal energy output peak in 1998.[6] Canada's peak came in 1997. The predicted peak for Chinese coal production is 2015, with supplies likely to be completely exhausted by the middle of the century.

Again, the idea that we have reserves to last 100 years assumes *current* rates of consumption. At current rates of *growth*—China's demand for coal rose 35 percent[7] between 2000 and 2006—we will have a coal shortage long before then. According to the IEA, global coal output will need to rise by more than 70 percent before 2030 to meet the growth in demand. Yet even a rise of 30 percent will bring a coal shortage. Nor do these predictions allow for any increase needed to reduce the impacts of declining oil reserves.

Even before we start trying to convert quantities of coal into oil, many scientists are predicting that the world's coal reserves will peak before 2025.[8] The US Energy Information Administration (EIA) says it will be in 2030.[9] That is not far away. If they are right, we face big troubles. It is likely that all the conventional oil may have gone by 2025. By 2045 all the coal may have gone too.

So finding enough coal to make up for the loss of oil, which is our largest source of energy, is not likely to be possible. Like oil, we have already used up most of the easily accessible coal—and the coal that is the best quality in terms of energy yield.

This means that although the use of non-conventional sources of oil is an option, it is not a very attractive or sustainable one. These resources will offer a stop-gap—and only once when we have built the capacity to develop them. And whatever we do, we face much higher fuel prices in the coming years as well as greater environmental damage by energy companies.

What about alternative fuels such as ethanol, electricity or hydrogen? Again, the outlook is not great. The history of alternative fuels for vehicles is largely a story of failures, at least so far.

One easy alternative to gasoline and diesel is liquefied natural gas. It is comparatively easy to modify existing engines to use it. Again, though, we risk running out of natural gas too, especially if we start using it widely as a transportation fuel.

As with oil, we have not found any major sources of gas since the 1960s. Our rate of use has exceeded what we have discovered each year since 1980. The US has already seen its gas production peak. The US Energy Information Administration (EIA) predicts that world gas production will peak in 2030,[10,11] although some forecasts are even less encouraging. Matthew Simmons and others believe that global natural gas production has already peaked.

Moreover, if we are already facing an oil shortage, surely there is a strong case to protect our remaining gas supplies for electricity and heat production, to make it last longer. We don't want to find new ways to use it, to fritter it away making unnecessary road trips too.

Natural gas is not a good long-term solution to the energy problem in the transportation sector.

What about biofuels? The most successful so far has been ethanol. This can be made from a wide range of sources of starch and sugar, such as fruit waste, potatoes, cheese whey, corn and sugar cane. The French even use low quality wine. And it is increasingly used as a substitute for gasoline, accounting for more than 5 percent of the world market in 2008. Almost all of this is produced in the US from corn and in Brazil, which has had a program since the 1970s, using sugar cane.

For now there is a technical limit to its use. American cars can only use gasoline containing a maximum of 10 percent ethanol, although this is being increased. In Brazil, cars and trucks are designed to cope with 25 percent; it also has a fleet of specialist vehicles that can use pure ethanol.

The problem is that a major shift in the use of ethanol for motor fuel would affect food prices and the amounts of food we could grow. In a world where our food supply is already problematic, and where we are facing water shortages too, this trade-off is not an easy one to feel comfortable about. Ethanol also needs much energy to produce.

Many regard Brazil as a model for what we can achieve, but it not an example that can be easily copied. Brazil's situation is unique. It has had an efficient low-cost sugar cane industry for decades and has learnt what works. It also has abundant land, although there are implications for the rainforests, and a perfect climate. No other country in the world benefits from such a favorable set of circumstances.

Indeed, there is no other country in the world where it makes sense to convert large amounts of sugar or starch crops into ethanol—including the US.

It is not cost effective, nor is it physically possible. American ethanol production was subsidized to the tune of $1.25 for every gallon produced in 2009. For corn ethanol to displace gasoline would need 120 percent of the country's crop land. It is impossible. The EIA thinks the limit for domestic ethanol production is about 700,000 barrels a day and that this level could be achieved by 2030. That would cut US petroleum demand by just 6 percent.[12]

Thankfully, there may be a partial solution in bio-waste products. We can make cellulosic ethanol out of unwanted bushes and trees growing on scrub land. We can also use switchgrass and crop residues. These can also be grown with much less need for fertilizers than food crops. They can be harvested more cheaply and grown on marginal land, instead of using rich farm land. There is a hope that cellulosic ethanol, or other hydrocarbons, can be produced using microorganisms digesting bio-waste or sugars in laboratories too. These may even make it possible to create a "drop-in" fuel, which can replace gasoline, diesel and aviation fuel directly, although this has not been commercially proven.

The uncertainty with cellulosic ethanol concerns the cost of processing (and for drop-in fuels, the cost of the sugars or enzymes). Because comparatively little effort has been put into either area, our understanding is still poor. The EIA thinks that cellulosic ethanol production costs may be five times greater than those associated with conventional corn ethanol production.[13] But validating this estimate is hard because the industry does not yet exist. That, in itself, says that cellulosic ethanol will not be available to offset the forecast decline in oil availability. Nor could it ever replace oil itself. The most ambitious plans of the US Department of Energy suggest that cellulosic ethanol could only replace 30 percent of America's 2004 petroleum needs by 2030. With less space to grow the bio-input, the opportunity in Europe is smaller still.

An important variation is biodiesel. About a quarter of the world's transport fuel is diesel and biodiesel is the only non fossil-based alternative. Biodiesel is relatively easy to make. It comes from animal fats and plant oils. Most of what is used today is derived from the oil discarded by fast food restaurants. Other common sources are soy beans and fish oil. Like ethanol, it can also be made in the laboratory, using algae and fungi, although neither of these methods has been proven commercially.

Biodiesel is used mainly in Europe where it accounted for 5 percent of the diesel-fuel market in 2010. Like ethanol, it is typically mixed with oil-derived diesel before use. The proportion of biodiesel in the mix can be raised when it is used in other applications, such as heating oil.

Biodiesel's potential is quite limited though. The exhaust fumes are carcinogenic and it does not perform well in cold temperatures. There is also a limited amount of restaurant oil that is discarded each day, which restricts the amount of biodiesel that can be produced this way. The alternative, using sources that are also foodstuffs, brings the same dilemma as with ethanol: Should we drive or eat? There is also the same problem with yields: vast amounts of land and fresh water would be needed to produce enough oil to completely replace conventional diesel fuels. In volume production, using soya oil, for example, it is also comparatively expensive.

What of the other renewables: wind, geothermal, solar and wave power? They will certainly help. They can be used to power homes and factories and cities. It is harder to use them for ships, aircraft and cars. But the electricity they produce could be used to create hydrogen or power batteries. Again, the problem is with capacity and time. Presently, about 85 percent of the energy we use comes from fossil fuels. While we may, one day, be able to replace this with wind or other renewables, we are a long way from that day. Solar power produced just 0.5 percent of the world's energy needs in 2008. Wind power was even less. While we can develop these sources, they cannot begin to meet our needs in the coming decades.

And while there has been grand talk of building giant fields of solar collectors across the world's deserts, these only offer a partial solution and carry many challenges too. Storing or transporting electrical energy in the quantities needed remains a technical hurdle that still has to be overcome. There are also political concerns. Europe, for example, is trying to become less dependent on imported energy, notably from Russia and the Middle East. Becoming dependent on power supplied from politically risky North Africa instead is only likely to swap one problem for another. Moreover, solar power delivery can be intermittent, is not available at night and depends on the vagaries of the weather. Finally, the time needed to build such farms, or negotiate their construction, is likely to be considerable.

What about increasing our use of electric cars, to reduce our dependence on oil? Well, this is possible and the cars are coming. The trouble is they are not coming fast enough because the technology is still far from ready. The cars that are available today are expensive, have limited range and take a long time to recharge. Their owners are said to suffer from "range anxiety," the fear that they will not make it to their destination. Today's electric cars are a long way from being realistic substitutes for their diesel or gasoline-fueled cousins.

Moreover, there remains the question of where the electricity will come from if we want to increase the electric vehicle fleet substantially. When the oil, natural gas and coal begin to run out we will lose much of the world's electricity-generating capacity. The cost of electricity will rise sharply. Nuclear power will be in short supply because there will not be enough nuclear plants to make up the shortfall. Building new ones takes decades and will require overcoming high social and political resistance in many countries. Hydropower will only be useful in places where dams can be built. Most critically, if there is already a shortage of power, will we want to use much of what we are still able to generate just moving around? It will be precious stuff.

We will use electric cars. But we cannot use 900 million of them—the number of vehicles using oil-derived fuel on the roads today. Nor can we use electricity to power aircraft or ships.

Finally, what about hydrogen, the "dream" source of power, the "hydro" in hydrocarbons? There is an almost unlimited quantity of the stuff. Powerful and clean, hydrogen-fed fuel cells could solve transportation problems, say the optimists. For electricity generation, hydrogen can be used to power massive turbines. It is the Holy Grail of energy.

Well, not quite.

The main problem is how to get the stuff. As every school child knows, one way is electrolysis. Two electrodes in a glass of water with a bit of power and the result is hydrogen gas as well as oxygen. But therein lies the problem. It takes energy. Where is that going to come from?

The main source of hydrogen today is natural gas and petroleum. Most of it is used to produce ammonia for fertilizers. Theoretically, the volumes produced in 2010 were enough to fuel about 40 million cars—about 4 percent of the world's fleet. But we cannot sustain a new hydrogen-based world by producing fuel from the materials we are trying to replace.

There are other methods of producing hydrogen—using corn ethanol, coal, oil sands, wood, wind and solar power, for example. But all depend on resources that are either running out, would use up food-growing land, or use science that is still, as yet, under developed.

There is also a problem about how to store and distribute hydrogen because it is so volatile. Additionally, using current technologies, it is extremely expensive to use. Fuel cells cost tens of thousands of dollars and much of the material that goes into manufacturing them, such as platinum, is in short supply. Hydrogen is simply not economically viable today. It will be at least thirty years before we can have any sort of developed hydrogen society.

But hydrogen *is* a long-term answer, assuming we can produce it efficiently, perhaps using nuclear power, while there is still enough uranium left, or by using some renewable source such as wind or solar power. It is a potential way to solve the oil crisis that we face. No other option approaches the magnitude of hydrogen's potential benefits. If only we had the understanding and capacity now.

Shine Some Light on the Problem

For the transportation sector, the biggest user of oil, there is no easy alternative to existing fuels that are likely to be available in sufficient time, in sufficient quantities and at a cost that is anything like comparable. Anyone who manufactures or uses cars, trucks, container ships and planes is facing a problem. And that means billions of us.

Without a clear alternative to oil we are going to have to make some changes to the way we live as our oil supplies begin to dwindle and prices rise. More than half of the oil burned is used to fuel aircraft, cars, buses and trucks. In the US it is more than two-thirds.[14] More than 60 percent in the growth in oil demand comes from the transport sector too.[15] A further 4 percent of our oil—3.2 million barrels a day—is also used to manufacture cars, trucks and planes.

We are going to have to learn to live using less oil. The changes need not be drastic at first, but they will be hard to get used to. One change, which will come quickly, is in car manufacturing. We will start to make much more fuel-efficient cars and trucks. We will also have to take fewer flights. Governments will cut speed limits and raise taxes on cars. Oil used by the military, for security, by the emergency services, in agriculture, for heating, and by trucks involved in essential delivery services, will have priority over that used for personal transport. Some regulators may even start to ration fuel, restricting the amount anyone can buy, so as not to penalize the poor.

Businesses most dependent on today's low cost energy will face a hard time. Instead of hundreds of courier and delivery services, there will need to be a consolidation to a few. Instead of driving around half empty most of the time, delivery vans will be used more efficiently. There will be more school buses and more grocery delivery services. We will begin to experiment with electric buses and taxis; vehicles where battery power makes much more sense because they return to base each evening and can be recharged overnight. There will be gradual restrictions on mobility in city centers, higher parking and road toll charges, all to restrict the consumption of oil-derived fuels. The motorization of the developing world will slow as fuel subsidies are removed.

Gradually, though, there will have to be bigger changes. The developed world has been transformed in the last 100 years by the availability of cheap oil. Buildings and cities have been designed with cars in mind. Motor vehicles have made it possible for us to live in the suburbs. We have built shopping malls in places that are impossible to reach without a car. Trucks deliver food to stores as well as mail and raw materials to factories. Ships move goods and fuel around the world. Aircraft have changed the way we travel and commute, especially in the last twenty years, since the birth of low-cost airlines.

Gradually, we will have to reverse this trend. Those with oil-fueled heating systems they cannot replace are going to have to change their spending priorities, start knitting or shiver. Those who work in air-conditioned offices, constructed out of steel with sealed-glass windows are going to have to change offices or start wearing shorts. People with fuel-thirsty vehicles will have to sell them, if they can find a buyer. Those who commute long distances will have to find another way to get to their offices or change jobs. The wealthier, those with weekend holiday homes a short flight away, will have to move there or give them up. Budget airlines will stop being called "budget." Ship owners will slow their journey times and put many of their ships in dock. Governments will squabble over the supplies that are left. More of us will learn to take the bus and the train.

International trade in many goods will decline. Flat screen televisions, shoes and jeans once made in China will be produced in Wisconsin, Bavaria or Western Australia instead, nearer their end markets. While this will provide much needed employment, easing the financial burden facing many people in the developed world, it will also affect the price. With fewer economies of scale, higher costs and smaller markets, the items produced may cost many times more than now.

With concurrent economic woes in many places, rising oil costs will accelerate the deflation of asset prices but inflate the cost of almost everything else. So we will see inflation rise for day-to-day items, as transport and power costs go up, and falling prices for big-ticket assets, like houses and second-hand cars, as people sell them off to fund their living expenses.

In the developing world regional airports will become even greater white elephants than when they were built. Many of the newly rich will be forced to return to the motorcycles and rickshaws they used before they bought cars. And around the world we will see bus services flourishing, although the ride will cost much more. Many people will learn to work from home, to telecommute.

There will be changes in electricity consumption too, many of them gradual at first. In malls and shops, lights will be turned off at night. So will street lights in towns and villages where they are not really needed. We will become much more energy conscious, wary about wasting the power we have left. We will turn to solar and wind power at home. Taxes on items that use large quantities of oil will rise. Ration coupons will help ease the transition and make it fairer. Black markets will spring up to profit from the shortages.

But using less gasoline and electricity will not solve the problem. Many other items we depend on, such as medicines, plastics and asphalt, all come from oil too. Few have easy or cheap substitutes. Products we barely think about will suddenly matter much more—such as ink, washing-up liquids, CDs, pesticides, deodorant, tires and ammonia. Many of the factories where we make these goods—and many others—are also powered by oil-derived fuels.

Air freighting fruit from far away places will become less viable, especially when it is likely to be sold to people who are struggling financially, burdened with debts and other price rises too.

For many people in the world, diets will get worse because they will need to consume cheaper foods with a lower nutritional content. Fruits and nuts will give way to breads and starches. In many countries, diets will return to the way they were in the 1940s. But rates of obesity may decline too, as foods become more expensive and so more highly valued.

In places where the land has been ruined by pollution or overuse, the ability to produce food will become a question of survival as the cost of fertilizer, fuel and transportation rise. And, for everyone, wherever they are, the price of disinfectants, many of the anesthetics and most of the medicines we need when we get sick will rise. As we will see in the next chapter, this has especially serious consequences.

All these changes will prolong our energy supplies, perhaps substantially. But they will also bring different standards of living and change the way our society develops. The loss of jobs, the loss of opportunity and the loss of wealth that will come with the end of oil supplies will not make for a happy world. Food inflation and food shortages will not make for a healthy one either. In the developed world, the middle classes will wonder what all their hard work was for.

For all of us, learning to consume less oil will be hard.

Endnotes

1. IEA World Energy Outlook Report, 2010. http://www.iea.org/index_info.asp?id=1479 See also http://www.chinadaily.com.cn/bizchina/2010-07/20/content_11023788.htm
2. Matthew Simmons, presentation on Twin Threats, Marsh's National Oil Companies' Conference 2010.
3. Ten years growth of 8 percent compound = 100 percent increase. So the amount we use will have doubled. As we have used half already, then that is the other half.
4. Founder of Ocean Energy Institute and ex-chairman of energy investment bank firm Simmons & Co Intl.
5. ASPO 2009 International Peak Oil Conference, October 12, 2009, Denver, Colorado, slide 34.
6. Actual production has risen since then but the quality—the energy output—of the coal has steadily declined.

7. "The great coal hole" by David Strahan, *New Scientist*, January 17, 2008.
8. Energy Watch Group, Coal, Resources and Future Production, *New Scientist* January 17, 2008, "Forecasting coal production until 2100," Mohr and Evans, University of Newcastle, Faculty of Engineering and Built Environment NSW, Australia: http://www.energybulletin.net/node/28287.
9. US Energy Information Administration: "International Energy Outlook 2008."
10. US Energy Information Administration: Table 5. World natural gas production by region and country, 2005–2030.
11. See also "Risk-opportunity analyses and production peak forecasting on world conventional oil and gas perspectives," Zhang et al, *Petroleum Science*, Volume 7, Issue 1, February 2010, pp. 136–146.
12. "Ethanol Makes Gasoline Costlier, Dirtier," Taylor and Van Doren, Senior Fellows of the Cato Institute. *Chicago Sun-Times,* January 27, 2007.
13. Cato Institute Study http://www.cato.org/pub_display.php?pub_id=7308.
14. US Energy Information Administration. http://www.eia.doe.gov/pub/oil_gas/petroleum/analysis_publications/oil_market_basics/demand_text.htm.
15. IEA "Reducing Oil, Consumption in, Transport: Combining, Three Approaches" April 2004 working paper.

11

WE WILL BECOME LESS HEALTHY

Happiness lies, first of all, in health.

George William Curtis

Human life expectancy has risen steadily for decades. On average, someone born today should live to the age of sixty-seven, although it varies greatly from country to country. In some parts of the developed world, the average lifespan has risen to more than eighty, while in the poorest parts of the globe it is still less than half that.

In almost every country, but not all, the number of years we live continues to rise. In the last fifty years, the average lifespan has risen by 29 percent.[1] Although the pace is slowing, the UN believes those born in 2050 will live nine years longer than those born in 2000 with the citizens of some developed-world countries expected to live to almost ninety, on average.

Such predictions come through extrapolating the data, of course. They take a trend line, which is well-established and has been known for decades, and then extend it into the future. Because medical care and nutritional standards have risen, because many fewer children die, and because we have eradicated many diseases, it makes sense to assume that this trend will continue.

But we know that the trend will not continue for ever. We know that the pace is already slowing. We are living progressively longer, but it seems that most of the big gains have already been made.

But what if the trend did not continue? What if it went into reverse?

There is good reason to think that it might. In essence, this is down to basic microeconomic theory; to the interaction between demand and supply. Demand for the things that keep us healthy, and allow us to live longer, such as decent food, medicines and disinfectants, is going to rise. Supply is, however, likely to be increasingly constrained by water and resource shortages. So the price of these items will increase, and many people will not be able to afford them as they can today. They will live less healthily, depend on cheaper food, and have less access to medical services when they need them.

Global demand for medical care will also rise because of larger populations. In China, Japan, Europe and parts of the US, aging populations will add to the demand for conventional health services. Climate change and economic stagnation in many places will increase the incidence of many diseases.

Because of budget constraints needed to reduce the levels of government debt, Western societies, as well as some of those in Asia, will find it hard to respond to this increase in demand for healthcare. So, again, the price of remaining healthy or of obtaining treatment will go up. Healthcare services and medicines will become more expensive too, favoring the rich. With poorer standards of healthcare for a larger proportion of the populous, illnesses that can be treated will become chronic or fatal for many people. For many millions, then, standards of living and health will fall.

Worse, unless we can find a way around these problems, life expectancies will begin to decline too—not just for the poorest few billion people in the world, but also for hundreds of millions who live in the developed world too.

Economic troubles are generally bad for our health. Typical recessions lead to higher rates of suicide and depression. Paradoxically, however, they also lead to a decline in the incidence of many other sorts of diseases or causes of death. The number of road accidents, the major cause of death for the young in most developed countries, tends to decrease. The incidence of liver and respiratory diseases usually falls too, so that overall, in the OECD countries, the mortality rate has actually declined in recent decades during times of economic hardship.[2] This is mostly explained by the provision of better social insurance and welfare services in the richer OECD nations.

However, economic troubles that are more serious and prolonged, that lead to steep cuts in welfare spending, or that have a long-term effect on income inequality, are very bad for our health.

Healthiness does not derive from absolute levels of economic power. Although the US is the biggest economy in the world, it has generally poor standards of health, on a par with those of sanctions-hit Cuba.[3] This is because America has a large proportion of very poor people without access to healthcare.

It is how the wealth is distributed that is important. In general, the more egalitarian a country, the smaller the gap between rich and poor, the healthier the population will be—as with Japan or the Nordic countries. This explains why Canadians are generally healthier than Americans.

Lengthy periods of economic hardship, which widen inequalities, are especially damaging to health standards. There was a marked decline in the levels of health after the Great Crash. Moreover, it takes a long time to repair the damage. Closing the health gap between rich and poor in the US after the 1920s took forty years.

One reason to worry about health levels in the future is because of the rise in income inequalities during the last thirty years. Since the 1970s, the gap between rich and poor has grown in many countries. Unrestricted free-market economic policies, notably in the US and some parts of Europe, have created wider income disparities than those that existed in the 1920s. Even before the 2007 correction, these were already evident in declining health standards. America's poor eat less well, have less access to medical care and, consequently, live shorter lives.

Given the depth of the financial problems facing much of the world, this trend is likely to accelerate and spread. Low health standards for the poorest people in the US, as well as rising levels of obesity and government budget constraints in many other Western countries, will make greater numbers of people less healthy than today. Even the most socially aware nations, such as those in northern Europe, will find it hard to fund their welfare and healthcare systems as generously as they have in the past.

How Much Oil Is in That Salad?

But budget constraints and wider income inequalities are only a small part of the problem. Another big issue is nutrition. Humankind's rising standards of health and longer life expectancy are primarily the result of access to energy. Oil has allowed us to lengthen the average time we live and to reduce the incidence of disease. As Al Bartlett, a professor at the University of Colorado, Boulder, puts it, "modern agriculture is the use of land to convert petroleum into food."[4]

Petroleum and natural gas provide many of the fertilizers we use to grow food. Oil-derived fuels drive the machines that make it possible to ship other fertilizers around the world, to harvest greater quantities of crops and transport them to the shops. They fuel many of our refrigeration systems. Oil is also an ingredient in many of the medicines we need to combat illness, and in the disinfectants we need to make our homes and hospitals safer.

Oil and gas make the growth and current survival of the world's population possible. Our discovery and ability to extract oil and gas in the last 100 years has had profound effects on our sustainability. In effect, hydrocarbons allow us to add 270,000 people to the planet every day. Take away oil and gas and our entire food system breaks down—or at least the scale at which it can be sustained disintegrates. A shortage of oil, and higher oil prices, will not be good for our health.

On average, every calorie we consume in the developed world needs ten calories of hydrocarbons. Some foods need much more. Industrially farmed beef needs thirty-five calories of energy just to put one calorie on a fork. It takes the equivalent of two liters of petroleum to produce a kilo of breakfast cereal, which will provide us with a fifth of the energy. Some crops are especially energy-hungry, notably those that are produced in the biggest quantities—wheat, rice and corn. Direct energy costs generally make up a smaller proportion of the costs for livestock farming, although, of course, the animals require feedstuffs, that are heavily dependent on both water and energy to grow.

So the food we consume today needs lots of energy. We think of that as coming from the sun and the soil. But modern farming needs much more energy than that. It needs energy to make the plants grow faster and in places where they would not naturally sprout. And it needs energy to power the huge machines that have allowed us to farm vast swathes of the world using many fewer people than in the past.

In today's high-tech farming, most of the energy used comes from ancient energy stores—from hydrocarbons. About 90 percent of the energy in crop production in the West comes from oil and natural gas. About one-third of this is used to reduce the labor input through the use of machinery. Another third is needed for fertilizers with the remainder needed for pesticide production, irrigation, drying, and other operations.

Not all of the fertilizer used is oil-derived, of course. As well as using natural gas, much also comes from phosphate deposits, mostly in the United States, Morocco, China, and Russia, as well as potash, which is mainly found in Canada, Russia, and Belarus. But these fertilizers also depend on oil to be transported from where they are mined to where they are needed.

The costs of processing and transporting food raises the amount of energy needed even more. America alone used energy equal to 1.75 billion barrels of oil in the agricultural sector in 2004 (see Table 11.1). A fifth of this was used to grow food, with the rest used to move, process, package, sell, and store it.

As in the transportation sector, this energy has been hopelessly under-priced for decades. Only because we have pushed so many of the costs of our energy use on to the environment and future generations have we have been able to expand food production to the levels we have today. Because modern economics has ignored so many of the externalities in the production of our food, it is much cheaper than it should be.

Table 11.1 United States Food System Energy Use

	Quadrillion Btu	Total Energy Use
Agricultural Production	2.20	21%
Transport	1.39	14%
Processing	1.68	16%
Packaging	0.68	7%
Food Retail	0.38	4%
Restaurants/Caterers	0.68	7%
Home Refrigeration/Preparation	3.25	32%
Total	10.25	100%

Source: *Earth Policy Institute*[5]

Note: *10 quadrillion British Thermal Unit (Btu) of energy is equivalent to 250 metric tonnes of oil or 1.75 billion barrels, nearly equivalent to France's annual energy consumption.*

With cheap food, we have produced more children than the planet can sustain. Food, which is subsidized by future generations, has actually encouraged us to breed too quickly, creating yet more mouths to feed, which has put even greater strains on the planet. If modern economics had functioned properly, the price of oil and gas would be much higher, so the price of food would be much higher, and the population would be much smaller. So, bizarrely, the failures of modern economics are actually responsible for the planet's over-population.

Another worry is that the huge growth in the use of chemical fertilizers in the last fifty years has been matched by a decline in the crop yields they have produced, although those appear to have stabilized more recently.

When energy shortages become more serious, the cost of the world's food will rise sharply. The continued use of natural gas for fertilizer is probably not much of a problem in the medium term. We only use about 5 percent of the world's gas to make fertilizers today. But the cost of using the farm machinery will rise, as will the costs of processing and transporting the fertilizers and food that is harvested. With demand for oil more constrained, demand for gas will rise, increasing the price of this too. Energy costs, which account for 15 percent of US farming costs today, will take a much bigger share.

All this means that the price of food will rise. For the poorest in the world, this raises the question of survival. For many others it will mean a switch to cheaper, less-nutritious diets, with a corresponding effect on health. Of course there will be benefits too. Those who are overweight will find it much cheaper and easier to eat less. Food will travel less, allowing us to eat what is locally produced too, so that the pleasures of seasonal fruits and vegetables will return.

Of course there are steps we can take as the costs of energy rise. We can return to rotating crops much more, to allow time for natural nutrients to return to the soils; we can use greater quantities of natural fertilizers and pesticides; we can develop ways to produce hydrogen for fertilizer using renewable energy; and we can return to a system with greater diversity, rather than growing food in vast monocultures, which tend to deplete soils faster.

As energy costs rise, farmers will gradually focus on crops that require less energy. We will be encouraged to eat more soya than wheat. Farmers will also adopt better soil conservation methods. Genetic scientists will develop seeds that need less water and less energy to grow. Storage will be improved, especially in much of the developed world. There will be less food waste as well as more efficient planting, harvesting and processing, especially in the developing world. There will be more jobs on the land again.

We will have to learn to eat less meat too. More than three-quarters of the grain produced in modern farms is used to feed livestock. While eating an apple gives us the energy held in the apple, feeding it to animals and then eating the animal, reduces the energy we receive by a factor of ten. The animal uses most of the energy from the apple itself. This calculation applies at each level of the food chain. So animals or fish that eat food that we could also eat, expend masses of energy before they reach our plates. This can make them hundreds of times less efficient to eat than a plant. In a resource-stretched world such calculations will begin to matter.

Thankfully, for the carnivores among us, this ten-to-one ratio does not always apply. A lamb or cow, which is fed on grass, or some other food that has not been fertilized and that we cannot consume ourselves, is not taking energy from us. It is converting the energy we need. So eating locally fed meat is much less problematic, at least from an energy efficiency viewpoint.

These changes will happen gradually and, certainly for those in the developed world, they will be barely noticeable for many years.

Our food prices will rise, there will be more locally produced fare in the shops and less that has been shipped around the planet. Food will, once again, account for a greater share of our spending. Diets will slowly change, with us consuming more starches, less meat and fewer eggs, for example. For some people this will bring health benefits.

But for the world's 2.7 billion poorest people, living on less than $2 a day, even small changes in the price of food threaten disaster. For tens of millions the prospect is one of starvation. Many face multiple threats, living in parts of the world that are expected to experience the worst water shortages and droughts. Rising sea levels and temperatures will make the plight of these people worse, increasing the risks of forced migration and disease. In many of the poorest countries soils are already badly degraded, with much of Africa facing an especially serious problem. Worse still, the availability of medical care has become increasingly difficult in many of these places already, as those who become doctors and nurses move away in search of better opportunities.

For those who are forced to remain in these countries, the prospects for their health and welfare are bleak.

For many, famine is the future.

I'll Give the Scalpel a Wipe Then

Higher energy prices will also affect the quality and price of medical care as well as the cleanliness of our homes and hospitals. Oil is used to make detergents, resins, fibers, certain lubricants, and gels. Petrochemicals are used in radiological dyes and X-ray films, as well as to produce syringes. Oil is the source of energy for much of a hospital's equipment, at least in some countries, and is the only source of power for the rescue helicopters and ambulances everywhere. It fuels the ships and trucks that move drugs around the world.

Petrochemicals are also needed for medicines, to manufacture analgesics, antihistamines, antibiotics, tranquillizers, antibacterials, suppositories, sedatives, cough syrups, creams, ointments and salves. Processed plastics made with oil are used in heart valves, intravenous tubing and oxygen masks. The coatings of pills, binders of tablets, ethanol solvents, sheeting, splints, blood bags, disposable syringes and catheters all depend on oil too.

So life without oil is going to get shorter for almost all of us, unless alternatives are found. In the meantime, the price of all these items will rise. This brings the risk that medical care will, increasingly, only be available to the rich or to those with insurance, and that we will come to live in a world where hospitals will be gated, protected by guards to keep out the poor.

Of course, there are other options and maybe even some benefits. We will learn to prescribe fewer, unnecessary drugs. A drop in the world's population will reduce the burden on the planet's resources. We can develop natural remedies and use more organic oils; after all, plants already provide a quarter of our medicines.[6] Several recently discovered drugs, including those to treat childhood leukemia, other cancers, weight loss and AIDS, have come from previously unknown species of plants that have been discovered in the world's rainforests. Others will surely be discovered.

Or at least they will be discovered if we stop burning the rainforests and destroying the world's ecosystems. We have already put 20 percent of the earth's plant species in danger of extinction. If we were to think holistically, if we were to appreciate that we will soon need replacements for the oil-derived medicines we use today, we would realize that this sort of destruction needs to stop.

Of course, it needs to stop for many other reasons too, not just because the world's plants may provide a future cure for many of the world's literal and metaphoric ills.

Was That a Cough?

An added concern is that the incidence of disease is likely to rise, partly from higher food prices, which will lead to declining standards of nutrition, at least for a few billion people. Some places will also see the increasing effects of years of heavy pollution on their health, as in the case of China and many other developing countries.

In China, cancer rates have risen by 80 percent during the last thirty years, chiefly because of higher levels of air and water pollution, as well as through contaminated food. Many of the vegetables consumed in the country are grown in soils tainted with heavy metals and other toxins. Pesticides are often used in dangerously excessive quantities too. In 2007, only 1 percent of China's 560 million city inhabitants were able to breathe air deemed safe by the European Union. Of the twenty most polluted cities in the world, sixteen are in China. The rivers and water systems are also in a poor state with 90 percent of China's sewage discharged, untreated, into them. As a result, drinking water often contains dangerous levels of arsenic, fluorine and sulfates and more than 600 million people have to drink water contaminated with human or animal waste. An estimated twenty million people drink well-water contaminated with high levels of radiation.

Although similar troubles afflict other developing countries China is worse off because it has a bigger population and has industrialized faster. The worry is that the effects of this will become more obvious in the years ahead. In 2009, China's death rate per 1,000 people was seven, slightly better than in the US,[7] which scored eight. (For comparison, most of Europe was ten while countries with younger populations like those in the Middle East have rates of four or five. Russia scores a woeful sixteen.) Although China's death rate fell during the 1990s due to rising prosperity, it has begun to rise again because of increased medical problems, one of the highest road fatality rates in the world, and an aging population. Between 2003 and 2009, China's death rate *increased* by 5 percent while average global death rates *fell* by more than 7 percent.

Road accidents have become a particularly serious problem in China, with more than 700 people dying on the country's roads each day and thousands injured. As the number of cars on China's roads grows, this problem will worsen—at least until the rising costs of motoring discourages car use.

A further health concern in many developing countries is the growing incidence of AIDS, a disease made worse in much of Asia by a lack of education and conservative attitudes about sex. It is already one of the biggest causes of death in low-income countries, according to the World Health Organization. Another problem comes from rising obesity levels, which means an increased incidence of diabetes and heart disease. Already, almost one in ten Chinese adults is affected by diabetes.

The incidence of disease will also rise because of climate change—although it is impossible to predict by how much. In all countries, the threat from pandemics, such as bird influenza, will remain a major concern. In developing countries, rising temperatures and humidity will mean more outbreaks of infectious diseases such as malaria, dengue fever and encephalitis.[8] Infectious and parasitic diseases are still one of the world's biggest killers, accounting for almost ten million of the sixty million human deaths each year,[9] and responsible for half of the annual deaths in Africa.

More frequent floods, desertification and droughts will make these troubles worse, adding diseases like cholera, tuberculosis and fatal digestive diseases to an already unhealthy mix. Diarrheal diseases are one of the leading causes of death in children in the developing world. The resulting higher death rates will also reduce economic activity and increase the burden on over-stretched medical systems. There is also likely to be a rise in geopolitical tension as a result of this suffering, which is dealt with in the next chapter.

In industrialized countries, higher levels of air pollution will make life harder for those with asthma, bronchitis, allergies, and heart conditions[10] because of higher pollen levels as well as more forest fires caused by climate change. Today, about 1.5 million people in Europe and the Americas die every year from respiratory problems. Heat waves also increase mortality rates dramatically, as illustrated by unusually hot summers in France and Russia in recent years when the daily death rate almost doubled.

The number of people infected with malaria, yellow fever and dengue fever is expected to rise in almost all regions of the world. Higher temperatures, more rainfall and higher levels of humidity will make it easier for mosquitoes to thrive.

Malaria is a major problem: already, 40 percent of the world's population is at risk with nearly 200 million new cases recorded every year. The proportion of those at risk is projected to increase to 80 percent by 2080.[11] In 2009, nearly one million people died of mosquito-borne diseases. That number is likely to rise steadily.

Rising temperatures affect the rate mosquitoes multiply, as well as the rate at which their salivary secretions become infected with pathogens. This means that mosquitoes are likely to re-infest countries where they have not been present in large numbers for several generations.

Although malaria has not been common in most European countries since the middle of the twentieth century, it has a long and difficult history in the region. Malaria was a major cause of death in Roman times and during the Dark Ages. The first archbishop of Canterbury, St Augustine, died of malaria after a trip to Rome. The famous English diarist Samuel Pepys, who died in 1703, also suffered from malaria thought to have been contracted after a series of unusually warm summers in Britain. Oliver Cromwell died of malaria in England in 1658, despite living through a time known as the Little Ice Age. Although the winters were unusually cold during this period, the summers were often unusually warm.

During the eighteenth and nineteenth centuries too, malaria was a serious problem in much of northern Europe and was endemic in Denmark.[12] In the second half of the nineteenth century, malaria infections began to decline in much of northern Europe, although Denmark still suffered devastating epidemics until the 1860s. Thereafter, the disease became relatively rare except during a short period following World War I.

The decline in malaria was due to improved drainage and the adoption of modern farming methods. Changes in demographics and living conditions were also important, as was the availability of improved medical care after the source of the disease had been clearly identified. Deliberate mosquito control did not really contribute to the decline, however, and malaria remained a problem in much of the Soviet Union as well as much of the US until the late 1940s. Dengue fever was also a problem in the US until the 1940s.

Again, the escalation of the occurrence of infectious, parasitic and respiratory diseases, which are expected to result from climate change, will affect the poor, the old, the weak and the young first.

The Buzz Has Gone

Climate change is also expected to affect adversely the life of many other insects, including pollinators. With an economic worth of only a few hundred billion dollars each year, pollinators seem fairly unimportant in the scheme of things. Yet bees, butterflies and bats, the main pollinators, are under threat: according to the US Department of Agriculture we face a pollination crisis.[13]

The UN Food and Agriculture Organization estimates that out of just more than 100 crop species, which provide 90 percent of food supplies for 146 countries, seventy-one are bee-pollinated, primarily by wild bees, while several others are pollinated by different insects and animals.

In recent years, the populations of many insects, bats and other pollinators, which have been falling steadily for some time, have started to plummet. Since the end of 2006 bee numbers have been devastated in many parts of the world by a disease known as colony collapse disorder (CCD). Some countries have had to import bees to pollinate their crops. In parts of China, some crops are now pollinated by hand. In 2008, Britain's farming minister told parliament that the country's bee population "could be wiped out in ten years"[14] unless something was done.

Something similar is happening to bats, which are also important pollinators as well as being large consumers of the more damaging insects we would rather not have. Around the world, a quarter of bat species are now listed as being in danger of extinction.[15] In the last five years, or so, colonies in the north and east of the US have also been affected by a previously unknown disease, called white-nose syndrome. (Interestingly, both white-nose syndrome and CCD were first found in the same year, 2006, although this may be entirely coincidental.) According to the US Fish and Wildlife Service, hundreds of thousands of bats have been found emaciated and dehydrated, with death rates among affected colonies at more than 90 percent. Unlike bees, bats have a very low birth rate, so the colonies will take decades to recover. Since it was discovered, white-nose syndrome has also spread further west and into Canada.

Although there is much less information on other pollinators, there is mounting evidence of problems with them too. The number of butterflies in Europe has fallen by 60 percent since 1990,[16] while in the US fifty-eight species of butterflies and moths, which are known pollinators, are now listed as endangered.[17] Of these, twenty-five are ranked "critically imperiled." The numbers of many species of small birds has fallen sharply too, with more than 10 percent of hummingbirds, also pollinators, now officially endangered.

Pollinators are known as "keystone" species. Just like the keystone in a building, the structure around them collapses if they are removed. More than 75 percent[18] of the 250,000 species of flowering plants in the world rely on these mobile animal partners to survive. Take pollinators away and crops of coffee, cranberries, blueberries, cotton, and hundreds of other goods we consume every day, will be devastated. A third of our diet depends on pollinated plants, including most of the healthy stuff. Other products like chewing gum, tequila and sisal, which is used for rope, rely on bats for pollination or seed dispersal. Without clover, alfalfa or soya, cattle and sheep farming would be harder too, threatening our supplies of beef, milk and leather. Moreover, our dependence on pollinated crops has been rising.

We would not starve in a world without pollinators because other foods, notably grains, could still be produced—assuming we can still fuel the tractors and fertilize the soil to produce them in sufficient quantities. But our diets would change radically without pollinators, and not in a good way. The loss of pollinators could also upset national trade balances, because supermarkets in the affected countries would be forced to import more food at a higher cost.

So far the cost of losing our pollinators appears to be small. Crop yields do not seem to have fallen, although there have been worrying signs in India recently. India accounts for 14 percent of global vegetable production.[19] But farmers have to pay more each year to rent bees, because the costs of antibiotics and replacing lost stocks keeps rising. The loss of other insects, as well as so many bats, has also resulted in a larger number of plant-eating pests. This means more is being spent on pesticides, which are one of the possible causes of CCD. More bees are also being shipped around the world, increasing the risk of spreading parasites and diseases. Others are being stolen.

According to the United Nations Food and Agriculture Organization,[20] pollination from animals, birds and insects was valued at $224 billion, or 9.5 percent of the value of the world's agricultural production for human food in 2005, with the fruits, vegetables and oilseed crops that are pollinated having a much higher value per ton than those that aren't.[21]

But these figures exclude the impact on other animals and are a small fraction of the costs that would be incurred if pollinators were to disappear entirely. Many plants that require pollination are important in the production of drinks, dyes, fuels, fibers and timber. They also supply medicines, especially in the developing world. Bats, which are the world's most numerous mammals, are voracious devourers of mosquitoes helping to protect many people, for the time being at least, from a range of nasty diseases including malaria and West Nile virus. Pollinated plants provide shelter for many animals too, while the fruits and seeds they produce are a major part of the diet of a quarter of all birds and mammals.

Addressing the decline in pollinators is hard, because scientists are unsure about the cause. More intensive farming, forest clearance, and habitat loss are certainly part of the problem. As well as pesticides, there is evidence that some mites and diseases are responsible too. Climate change is modifying the flowering cycles of many plants and the migration patterns of birds, and hibernation patterns are being disturbed, so these factors may play a role too. Air pollution is blamed in some places, while mobile phone signals are said to confuse the navigating capabilities of many insects and birds. Wind farms are known to be harmful to bats, especially when they are migrating.[22] And, as might be expected, there is suspicion about the effects of genetically modified crops as well.

Perhaps the biggest concern, though, is that we know so little about what is really occurring. In a statement[23] by the National Academies to the US Congress, Professor May Berenbaum, the head of the committee charged with looking into the decline of pollinators, said, ". . . it is difficult to think of any other multi-billion-dollar agricultural enterprise that is so casually monitored. It is astonishing how little we know about something so critical to our existence."

This is something we need to change.

It is perhaps a large step to suggest that these troubles will lead to falling life expectancies across the world. Yet the omens are not good. Healthcare will cost more almost everywhere; the cost of nutrition will rise; the incidence of diseases will rise; and, at the same time, the demands on the medical systems in Europe, Japan and China will increase due to aging populations.

Moreover, the impact of these changes will come at a time of economic constraint in many countries, with healthcare budgets under pressure. We will be faced with a stark choice—to increase spending on hospitals and medical care, or accept greater levels of ill health and declining life expectancies.

Government decisions on healthcare spending will also have to be set against many competing demands.

As we will see in the next chapter, one of those will be an increased need to provide higher levels of security and defense.

Endnotes

1. United Nations, Department of Economic and Social Affairs, *World Population Prospects: The 2006 Revision*, New York 2007.
2. "The effect of economic recession on population health," Stephen Bezruchka MD MPH www.cmaj.ca on August 31, 2009.
3. Spiegel JM. "Daring to learn from a good example and break the 'Cuba taboo.'" *International Journal of Epidemiology* 2006; 35: p. 825–6.
4. "Forgotten fundamentals of the energy crisis," *Journal of Physics*, 46(9), 876–888, Bartlett, A. A. (1978), p. 800.
5. Earth Policy Institute M. Heller and G. Keoleian," Life-Cycle Based Sustainability Indicators for Assessment of the U.S. Food System," Ann Arbor, MI: Center for Sustainable Systems, University of Michigan, 2000, p. 42.
6. "The World Conservation Union's Red List of Threatened Plants," 1998. IUCN, International Union for Conservation of Nature, Cambridge 1999. See also *New Scientist*, "Medicines from the Rainforest," August 17, 1991.
7. CIA, *The World Factbook*, 2010.
8. "Effects of global climate change on disease epidemics and social instability around the world," Huei-Ting Tsai, Tzu-Ming Liu, Department of Epidemiology, University of North Carolina, UN Human Security and Climate Change International Workshop, Norway, June 2005.
9. Disease and injury regional estimates for 2004, WHO, table DTH6.
10. US Center for Disease Control and Prevention – various reports. See also "Effects of global climate change on disease epidemics and

social instability around the world," Huei-Ting Tsai1, Tzu-Ming Liu, Department of Epidemiology, University of North Carolina at Chapel Hill; Human Security and Climate Change Workshop, Holmen Fjord Hotel, Asker, near Oslo, 21–23 June 2005; and EPA Regulations on Air Contamination, 2010.

11. Sachs and Malaney 2002; Department for International Development 2004.
12. "Climate Change and Mosquito-Borne Disease," Paul Reiter, *Environmental Health Perspectives*, Volume 109, Supplement 1, March 2001.
13. US Fish and Wildlife Service, Recommendations for Minimizing Pesticide Impacts to Pollinators, July 2006 http://www.fws.gov/contaminants/Pollinators.cfm, See also, Ingram, M. G.P. Nabhan, S. Buchmann. 1996b. "Impending pollination crisis threatens biodiversity and agriculture." *Tropinet* 7: 1.
14. *WalesOnline*, "Parasite could 'wipe out our honey bees within 10 years,'" March 25 2008 Steve Dube http://www.walesonline.co.uk/countryside-farming-news/countryside-news/2008/03/25/parasite-could-wipe-out-our-honey-bees-within-10-years-91466-20668112/.
15. Bat Conservation Trust, Bats of the world, 2010 http://www.bats.org.uk/pages/bats_of_the_world.html.
16. The European Butterfly Indicator for Grassland species: 1990-2007, European Environment Agency, October 2008, http://www.bc-europe.org/upload/VS2008-022%20European%20Butterfly%20Indicator%201990-2007.pdf.
17. Risk governance of pollination services, International Risk Governance Council , Geneva 2009 sourcing Xerces Society, Red List of Pollinators Insects of North America, 2005 www.xerces.org/Pollinator_Red_List/index.htm.
18. "Pollinators in Natural Areas: A Primer on Habitat Management," Black Hodges, Vaughan and Shepherd. Kremen et al, 2007.
19. Study by University of Calcutta's Ecology Research Unit, presented by Parthiba Basu at British Ecological Society meeting, University of Leeds, August 2010.
20. Food and Agriculture Organization of the United Nations, "New ecosystem approach based project: wild pollinators for food production." http://www.fao.org/agriculture/crops/news-events-bulletins/detail/en/item/7588/icode/?no_cache=1. See also *ScienceDaily,* Economic Value Of Insect Pollination Worldwide Estimated At U.S. $217 Billion," September 15, 2008.: http://www.sciencedaily.com/releases/2008/09/080915122725.htm.

21. *ScienceDaily,* "Economic Value Of Insect Pollination Worldwide Estimated At U.S. $217 Billion, "September 15, 2008. http://www.sciencedaily.com/releases/2008/09/080915122725 .htm.
22. David Biello, "On a Wing and Low Air: The surprising way wind turbines kill bats," *Scientific American,* August 26, 2008. http://www.scientificamerican.com/article.cfm?id=wind-turbines-kill-bats. See also Wendy Williams, "When Blade Meets Bat: Unexpected bat kills threaten future wind farms," *Scientific American,* February 2, 2004. http://www.scientificamerican.com/article.cfm?id=when-blade-meets-bat.
23. May R. Berenbaum, "Colony Collapse Disorder and Pollinator Decline," statement before 110th Congress (First Session), March 29, 2007. http://www7.nationalacademies.org/ocga/testimony/Colony_Collapse_Disorder_and_Pollinator_Decline.asp.

12

WE NEED TO DIFFUSE THE THREATS OF CONFLICT

War does not determine who is right—only who is left.

Bertrand Russell

It is comforting to think that arms are needed only for hugging. Sadly, they are also necessary for fighting battles, subduing the angry, and cowing the desperate.

Although we might all hope there will be fewer sources of conflict in the years to come, there is good reason to think that the number of battles between the peoples of the world will increase. And, while Western politicians have frequently exaggerated the need for recent wars, the conflicts of the future are likely to seem more justified. Of course, the problems facing humankind cannot be solved by military action, riots or chaos. But that will probably not stop people trying.

There are many potential reasons for wars to break out in the years ahead, and almost all have historical precedent, in the sense that they have been used to justify previous conflicts too. The exception to this is climate change. While there have been many wars fought over access to fertile land, natural resources and water in the past, none were of the potential scale we now face. As sea levels rise, hundreds of millions of people will lose their homes and their means of survival. They will be forced to migrate to places they are not keen to go and are unlikely to be welcome.

The tensions concerning declining resources will have an intensity not seen before, because the number of people fighting for their share has never been so large. As the world's supplies of oil, water, copper and tens of other resources come under strain, as demand exceeds supply, and as prices rise, there will inevitably be fighting over what is left. Countries will put up barriers to stop exports of their dwindling supplies resulting in trade wars too. And, as food prices rise, billions will fight to avoid starvation. In the developed world, millions more will demonstrate against the loss of jobs, cuts in welfare payments, declining standards of healthcare services, and the loss of promised pensions.

Humankind will wage some, or all, of these battles in the coming decades, unless we can do something clever and creative to prevent them; unless we can diffuse these threats; unless we can turn off the road we are on. The battles will be between the haves and have nots, as well as between the haves and have mores, as George W. Bush might have said. There will also be a great deal of friction between the public and private sectors leading to rising political uncertainty.

We are not dealing with soft issues here. We are dealing with changes that determine our ability to live, to have our sons and daughters prosper. The difficulty of the struggle is perhaps best understood in the words of George Kennan. In 1948, as head of the US State Department planning committee, he wrote about America's new found role as the dominant force on earth:

> We have about 50% of the world's wealth but only 6.3% of its population. . . . In this situation, we cannot fail to be the object of envy and resentment. Our real task is . . . to maintain this position of disparity without positive detriment to our national security. To do so, we will have to dispense with all sentimentality and day-dreaming; and our attention will have to be concentrated everywhere on our immediate national objectives. We need not deceive ourselves that we can afford today the luxury of altruism and world-benefaction. . . . The day is not far off when we are going to have to deal in straight power concepts.
>
> —GEORGE KENNAN

We Do Things Differently, Don't You See?

One of the earliest sources of renewed international tension will come from the financial crisis. It already has. Like a pendulum swinging back, world trade will become less open in the coming years. After decades of effort to build a globalized world, of deals signed to reduce barriers to cross-border business, the great weight will swing in the other direction again, just as it has in the past. Capital controls, already back in fashion, will return more broadly, and eventually trade sanctions too. Currencies will become favorite battlegrounds, as will the great shipping lanes along which goods move to and fro. Countries will accuse each other of subsidizing trade, manipulating their currencies and of competing unfairly. Politicians will play to the voters' gallery, offering protections for jobs and investment, and a vanquished foe, in return for re-election.

This is bad for the world, as Smith identified. It is usually better for countries and regions to specialize in what they are good at and to trade with each other. That creates more prosperity and leads to greater social well-being for all those involved.

It is also, unfortunately, logical and natural to close the barriers to trade and investment when times get tough. It is hard for a US president, or any other Western political leader, to resist the pressures to restrict Chinese or other foreign imports when the consequences of these imports, albeit maybe only in the short term, are more welfare payouts and higher unemployment at home. That is a tough political "hot potato" to sell when there are many softer and colder ones in the bag.

So, just as in the 1930s after the Great Crash when there was a gradual closing down of world trade, at least in part, we can expect much the same in the years to come. More racism will come with it, more nationalism too. That is natural enough too, it seems.

But there will also be a new and different battle over economic ideology. Big businesses in America and Europe compete in a different way from big businesses in China. This is not just a question of costs, but also of business models. Both sides see their own model as being fair. Both see the other side's model as wrong.

In the West, a business is expected to survive independently. It is expected to raise finance, compete for resources and people, build a customer base and then make a return, a profit, which is enough to reward its shareholders and to reinvest in the business for the future. Businesses that fail to achieve this balance go bust.

In China, the model is mostly different, partially because of the legacy of the country's communist past. There, big businesses are often state controlled, or at least state directed. Profit is less of a motivating factor, or at least that is not the sole reason why they are in business. They are led, or directed, centrally by the Party, with senior managers often moved between domestic competitors on the orders of Beijing. They may have shareholders and listings on stock exchanges, but the reward for investors is meant to come mainly from how well they gamble on the market. Their customer base is often provided: in the Chinese rail business, for example, new contracts are only offered to local companies, to ensure skills and jobs and wealth are kept at home, not sucked away by foreign-devil employers. Their technology is often provided too, removing the need for hefty research and development (R&D) costs. "Leached" away from foreign companies, and then localized, Chinese companies have frequently acquired their high technology capabilities without the costs. And when Chinese companies go abroad, the state is behind them, like a hand inside a puppet. It helps them gain access to the world's resources. When they make a bid to build new roads, schools or railways in California, Africa or Eastern Europe, the Chinese state, or one of its banks, will provide the client with low-cost financing, while Chinese companies will provide the low-cost labor, making it impossible for rival European or US bidders to compete.

For China, these are strategic investments, a way to beat their opponents in business and win geopolitical influence at the same time. Western companies say it is unfair competition.

Despite the complaints of many American and European politicians and business people, the Chinese model is not wrong. It is just different. It does not depend on the free market and profit to survive. It takes a different approach, and perhaps a better one. For the last thirty years, the unrestricted free market was the mantra of the West. Many business leaders in the West were even fooled into thinking that this was the only way to compete, the only way to achieve growth and economic superiority. Not only have Western businesses suddenly discovered that their model does not work as well as they once thought, they are about to find out that there is another way to compete that will undermine their system further still.

This will raise all sorts of trade tensions in the years to come and lead to a sharp growth in East-West rivalry.

Such tensions risk reawakening other sources of strife between peoples too. As German Chancellor Angela Merkel said in a speech in 2010, there is a growing awareness that multiculturalism has not worked[1]—that the integration of races and peoples of many nations to live harmoniously together has "utterly failed."

If this is the conclusion after fifty years of hard work in integrating people in one of the more open and liberal nations on earth, the risks of greater trade and business rivalry will only fuel the flames of division further. These risks will have two other consequences that will act together as a catalyst to make tensions worse still.

When trade barriers rise, when divisions between races and nations grow, when there is more distrust and more nationalism, then economic activity tends to slow. With that comes higher unemployment and, for those countries that have become too heavily dependent on foreign imports, higher costs. They will suffer from inflation, as local companies without the scale and cost advantages try to provide alternatives to goods previously imported. With inflation comes yet higher social discontent, as the spiral unwinds, spinning backwards again after so many decades. This typically fuels further nationalism and spreads the desire for isolationism wider still.

The second consequence is political. As the growth slows, and misery and anger mount, as countries shut down again, politicians will emerge from the shadows with simple answers and an inviting, but extreme, left- or right-wing rhetoric. They will appear to offer some false road to a better place, which will be wrong again, just as it was in the past.

The world moves in cycles—economically, socially and politically. Without care, our current world risks moving into reverse in all three.

The Cupboard Will Soon Be Bare

Another source of conflict will be about water, food and other vital resources. For years we have lived by exploiting the resources we can and thinking, thanks to faulty economics, that we can pass most of the external costs on to future generations.

Now the bill is coming due for payment.

According to the World Wildlife Fund[2] (WWF), our demands on the world's natural resources doubled between 1966 and 2007. Worse, with the population rising, the rate of overuse is accelerating. We are already living 50 percent beyond the earth's capacity, and by 2030 we will need a second planet if we carry on living as we do today. If everyone used resources at the same rate per person as the United States, we would need four and one-half planets. According to Jim Leape, Director General of WWF, the "developed world is living in a false paradise, fueled by excessive consumption." Some think the situation is even worse. David Pimentel, an expert on food and energy at Cornell University, says that if the entire world consumed the same way as the United States, humanity would exhaust its fossil-fuel reserves in less than a decade.

With the growth trajectory of many developing nations, notably those with large populations like China and India, this does not add up. Either the West has to change its consumption habits, or developing nations will not be able to develop much further. There is a crunch coming, which will become apparent long before 2030. Something has to give.

How this will manifest itself is hard to predict. There is likely to be friction regarding access to rivers and aquifers, as well as access to land to grow crops. The arguments in favor of growing food for biofuels will weaken. Countries are likely to introduce limits on food exports, stock-piling for security. Many governments may use their control over resources to win geopolitical influence. When China's Deng Xiaoping pointed out that "the Middle East has oil. China has rare earths," he was not making a simple observation. It is not only knowledge that brings power; rare earths, oil, and many other items essential to our standard of living or survival, can too.

We can also be reasonably sure that there will need to be changes in the diets of millions. For some, this will be voluntary. In the developed world more people are likely to choose to eat less meat, perhaps as a result of images of the less-fortunate in the developing world. In most places, though, dietary changes will come as a result of the price. Millions will have to eat cheaper food.

Tensions are also likely to rise domestically in many countries, with the likelihood of more Malthusian moments over shortages of tortilla flour in Mexico, as well as riots over rice in Africa or *kim chi* price protests in South Korea.

The shortages of food and water will also have an international business dimension. In the last decade, purchases of land in developing countries by developed-country organizations to grow food, have grown ten-fold according to the World Bank. Two-thirds of these purchases have been in Africa, where there has been a generally weak institutional defense. As well as government-sponsored purchases from Asia and the Middle East, there have also been substantial investments by hedge funds, and other financial companies, keen to make a profit from the anticipated shortage of land and food in the future. Big global finance businesses have quietly invested billions of dollars in the last few years, not to grow food, but to speculate on good quality arable land with access to water in these places.

Both motives are likely to bring trouble in the future. African and other developing-country governments will tire of their land being exploited by others, with their harvests being shipped off for the citizens of other countries to consume. Many of the citizens of these countries are also likely to rebel against the desire of others to profit from the vital elements needed for their survival. Legislative barriers stopping these sorts of investments will rise.

Brazil has already passed a decree to limit the amount of land that can be owned by foreign companies, while Argentina, which is already 7 percent owned by foreigners, is drawing up similar plans. As prices rise and people starve, there will be a growing realization among many governments that their land is not a commodity that can be easily bought and sold for the benefit of people overseas, even including a handful of bankers. Absentee landlords who buy and sell chunks of the earth for exported gain risk having their investments confiscated.

One partial solution to these problems is to increase the production of food in countries where there is lots of land and water, and where productivity levels today are still comparatively low.

There are a surprising number of places where this is possible. In parts of Africa, such as Congo and Sudan, in much of South America, as well as in Ukraine and Russia, there are vast areas of land that could be turned over to crop production. Climate change may also extend the capacities and productivity of other northern countries to grow crops, although it is also likely to reduce yields in places near the equator.

In many countries that have the potential to raise crop yields, however, there are obstacles. In parts of South America, Asia and Africa, the development of new crop land would require further destruction of the rainforests. In many countries too, there would need to be social change to allow the establishment of a high-volume agricultural sector, which would take time. Moving from a system of small-holdings to one with large mechanically-farmed fields and a developed transport infrastructure does not happen quickly. There are also concerns about the future cost and availability of fertilizers in some places, as well as political hurdles in some African countries still affected by civil war.

Even so, countries with the capacity to export more food are likely to gain geopolitically, with few having as much opportunity as Russia. Not only does it (and many countries within Moscow's sphere of influence) have great potential to increase grain production, it has huge reserves of oil and gas too. Russia and much of the Commonwealth of Independent States (CIS) also have vast supplies of water and fertilizer. Indeed, Russia has the potential to become one of the great powers of the twenty-first century, if it can reform its agricultural sector and maintain its energy supply network. Moreover, climate change may actually be good for Russia. It will increase the amount of land that can be farmed and also provide easier access to oil and gas fields that currently lie under deep permafrost.

There is, of course, considerable irony here. Not only will the means of competition in the business world be challenged by China's communist ideology, but the ability of the West to wield geopolitical power will be challenged by what it once saw as a defeated communist foe in Russia. In some ways it will seem as if the Cold War never ended.

Perhaps the biggest source of change in the balance of geopolitical power, however, will come because of access to oil and other sources of energy. Many African states, long manipulated by Western powers wanting to access their resources or to fight proxy wars on their territory, will find their position strengthened by the arrival of additional Chinese, and perhaps even Indian, investors in their countries. Local African politicians and business people with the skills may be able to play the West off against the newcomers and gain much in return. On past records, however, this is unlikely to lead to a general improvement in social welfare or the well-being of many African citizens. Nor is it likely to improve standards of education, health or human rights. More probably, unfortunately, the gains will accrue to a minority, wealthy elite. But the power of the West to set the price for oil, uranium and tens of other resources could also be compromised, forcing up prices.

Many organizations have undertaken studies into peak oil and the consequences of these shifts in geopolitical power, including the US military and Lloyds insurance. A 2010 study by the German military[3] suggests there will be significant shifts in loyalties. It says we risk a fall in the influence of "Western values" and deteriorating standards of human rights, combined with a greater tolerance of rogue behavior and a rise of more oil-related diplomacy. Out of necessity, the risk of moral hazard and extreme political tensions will grow, making the world more volatile, unless we handle the transition from our current oil dependence with great care. With gas an obvious alternative to oil for applications other than transport, the security of pipelines is also likely to become ever more problematic, says the German report. Those supplying the gas will have even greater opportunity to hold their customers to ransom, while terrorists or the disaffected will have more chance to create havoc by blowing them up.

Other conflicts are almost inevitable over territorial disputes, notably in much of Asia and the Arctic where there are longstanding disagreements. Most of these concern islands where oil, gas and other mineral reserves are believed to exist. In several cases more than two countries have staked claims, suggesting these could get diplomatically messy. They will also test the limits of soft power in the Pacific and settle, for a generation at least, the argument about which government is in charge. Will rising China, waning Japan or the US, with a long history of power-broking in the region, prevail?

As the supply of oil becomes more of a problem, the risks from nuclear technology will also grow. Although it will take time to construct the capacity, this source of power will become a necessity for many nations. Critical to how this will evolve and what it will mean, is how governments react to the energy gap—the time between the early effects of an oil shortage beginning and the day when reliable long-term alternatives, such as nuclear power, are available in sufficient quantities. The gap could last more than a decade.

Building lots of nuclear power stations also brings additional domestic, regional and international threats. Statistically, the risk of accidents will grow. There will be political battles between those in favor of their construction and those deeply opposed. There is also the issue of waste. And even then, nuclear power does not solve one of the main problems that will result from the eventual decline in oil reserves; airplanes and cargo ships cannot be powered by batteries or reactors—or at least not yet.

During the gap, there will also be a source of local conflict in many countries about the choice of whether to grow food for fuel or to eat. In some places constraints on water availability and the effects of soil degradation will add to the complexity.

The early effects of peak oil will also result in the politicians and citizens of many countries demanding greater local autonomy over their sources of energy. This may not be realistic or possible in many countries, but that will not stop people trying. Many countries will over-invest in solar, wind, geothermal and other energy sources in an attempt to wean themselves off oil and to reduce the power and political influence of countries with large gas and oil supplies. The stakes on all sides will be high.

In all this, according to the German military report, governments will take a much greater role in society than today, and the influence of the private sector will decline. In the major energy supply countries this will be necessary to consolidate political power. In the countries that have to import energy, it will be to try and ensure a fair allocation of resources and stop private sector manipulation or profiteering.

As a result, more resources and exploration activities will be nationalized and licenses already given to energy companies risk being revoked. According to the German report, however, private enterprises will gain in some places. They will still be needed to protect the energy supply infrastructure and ensure production and transportation security in less developed regions, where threats of conflict or terrorism are expected to grow.

In the face of so many pressures, the need for regional and international cooperation will obviously increase; however, history suggests that attempts at peaceful negotiation, when the stakes are so high, will have little success. Although there will be a need for global institutions to intervene, the German report suggests that the opposite will happen—that bodies such as the UN, OPEC, and even the EU, risk becoming less influential as local and domestic solutions take priority.

Faced with such challenges, some governments will see a greater incentive to meddle in the political affairs of energy-rich rivals, in an effort to influence their decisions about whom to supply. Such games will inevitably turn nasty in some places, where those who need the oil and gas try to take effective control of the countries that supply it. Countries particularly vulnerable to these types of maneuvers include many of those in Africa, Central Asia and Venezuela—countries rich in reserves but weak in geopolitical clout. With so many interested parties, the governments of these countries may have more influence, but they will also be subject to much greater external pressure.

Peak oil and the battles for the world's declining natural resources also carry systemic risks. The impact of resource shortages, especially energy, may be much less gradual than we would like to imagine. According to the German military study, the effects could be linear.

Oil and market-driven economies, such as the US and much of Europe, risk a rapidly evolving chain reaction of events. What could begin as a relatively slow decline in trade and economic activity could accelerate quickly. As resource shortages hit, prices would rise and economic activity would slow. Unemployment would go up. Government budgets, already under strain, would be weakened further, with higher welfare demands, lower tax receipts, and the burden of investing in alternative technologies. Established supply chains for food and other items, so closely and tightly linked around the world, would begin to disintegrate. Financial markets would not fare well, nor would currencies. Over a matter of years, says the study, such resource troubles could lead to the collapse of many economies, mass unemployment, government defaults and infrastructure breakdowns, ultimately followed by famines and total system collapse.

None of this is a cheery prospect but, surely, it is horrid enough to make us act in advance.

It risks beginning within a decade.

But You Promised!

The third major source of conflict between peoples is likely to come *within* countries rather than between them. In the West, the sense of discontent is likely to grow among citizens as years of spending restrictions, needed to reduce the debts accumulated in the last thirty years of over indulgence, cut deeper.

In Japan, more than twenty years of economic decline since 1990 have had little effect on social stability. Unfortunately, it is unlikely to be the same elsewhere. Few nations are as stoical as the Japanese. Few will have the ability to invest in infrastructure and provide jobs, as Japan could. Few have populaces with plenty of savings, as Japan had. And almost none will be able to maintain even stagnant rates of economic growth through exports, as Japan did.

As a result, we are likely to see more demonstrations similar to those seen in Greece, Iceland, Ireland, Latvia and France in 2010, where law and order breaks down, at least temporarily. There will be more acts of social rebellion too, with a refusal to pay taxes and the growth of black economies. Cash will be king.

The citizens of many Western countries will be confronted by a dizzying number of additional financial challenges at the same time. They will find their taxes rising and their incomes falling, as governments try to balance their books and economic activity slows. The value of their investments and savings will drop, while the prices of goods and services will rise, partly from currency movements, but also from resource shortages. Pension payouts will be cut, health insurance and motoring costs will rise and the value of their homes will stagnate or fall further. The cost of servicing their loans will go up. For almost everyone, money will be in short supply, and many of those brought up in a world of immediate gratification will be shocked by what the changes mean. It will make many of them angry too.

For the middle classes of the West, the outlook is much the same as it is for the poor, possibly worse. Many will face longer hours of work and longer working lives for less pay. They will have to replenish their savings. They will have less to spend and what they do have will not go as far as before. They will not be able to afford to keep their second homes or even get to them, as the cost of aviation fuel rises, and their disposable incomes fall.

Of all these troubles, the worst may be the broken promises. Many Western citizens face the failure of pensions' funds, both state-backed and private, to do what they once said they would do. Instead of looking forward to long and happy retirements, many face working well into old age, or short retirements with little cheer. When they get sick, their healthcare insurance will not offer as much cover as they once believed it would either. Those depending on state-backed medical care, mostly in Europe, will see service levels decline, as spending cuts and aging populations overload the system.

The West will need to boost its domestic security apparatus in response to these woes, for this discontent will bring anger, resentment and calls for radical political change. There will be a need for more police on the streets and increased security to repel threats from domestic terrorists and cyber criminals, intent on causing seditious damage in revenge for what they will see as so many injustices. This will come at a time when many armies and police forces will be faced with their own budgetary cutbacks and their own sense of betrayal. Instead of supporting their political masters, they may turn against them, at least in the most extreme cases.

The thin veneer of civilization is not that thin. But it is thin, nonetheless.

Climate Change Will Bring Threats of Conflict Too

Finally, there is climate change. When US President Barack Obama collected his Nobel peace prize he said that climate change "will fuel conflict for decades." This statement was not a political one nor was it based on the findings of scientists. It is the view of US military generals.

Certainly, the turmoil that is likely to result from floods, storms, rising sea levels and drought, will not make us any happier. Some forecasters are especially apocalyptic, predicting the end of the Indian monsoon, the loss of many parts of the habitable world and state failure in some places. The next report from the UN's Panel on Climate change, due in 2013, will include a specific chapter on the threats to human security from changes in sea levels and temperatures.

At this point, when any predictions are still so speculative, it is impossible to say what climate change will mean to humanity. But from what has been published to date we can be reasonably sure already, that the modern world has never faced problems on the scale anticipated. We know that climate change may bring benefits for some of us. Just as the Norwegians once grew grape vines, the melting Siberian permafrost will allow easier access to Russian energy reserves. But we also know that drought caused the end of the Mayan civilization, and that Europeans had to abandon their settlements in Greenland when temperatures fell. We know too, that rising temperatures are likely to bring crop failure and economic decline for many countries, especially those that are heavily dependent on agriculture; this means parts of Africa, where the likelihood of conflict due to climate change is expected to rise.

Perhaps the hardest outcome will be the growing realization that our children will probably pay an even higher price than us for our folly. Although most of those alive today will pay part of the bill for our own short-term thinking, over-exploitation of the planet's resources and greed, future generations are likely to pay more. They will be left with most of the debts. They will have to find new medicines and fertilizers to prevent life expectancies falling and to replace the ones we will have used up. They will have to find alternative sources of power for transportation. They will have to work out what to do in a world with rising temperatures, depleted rainforests and plundered oceans. We cannot fix the problems we have created in a generation, especially when many of them are still getting worse.

This is a tragedy. Our children should be the ones to take us forwards, in to the future. For each of us, they are our genes of potential immortality. But unless we make radical changes soon, or come to a grand global agreement to manage the world better, our children will be left to fight wars over energy, water and food. Our legacy to them will be economic decline, social stagnation and conflict. While once there were enlightened ideas, plans for our species to explore the edges of the universe, reach for our intellectual boundaries and glory in our artistic wonders, we risk leaving them a shrinking, shattered world. Without change, grand ideas will be for another age, not the one to come. Not for them.

There will be many battles to come. Even when we have started to respond to the problems we have created, to change the way we live, there will be battles over money, water, land, fuel and food. There will be struggles over ideology. Dangerous new political parties will spring up. We will fight about religion, race, and law, and about the dwindling rights of humankind.

But the biggest battle of all that we will fight is perhaps the least obvious one today. We may fight to win resources, or struggle to keep our homes, we will argue in denial or fumble for different options through repentance, but the fight that we will remember most will be the one we do not yet see. And it is the one that we all will lose.

It is the fight about who to blame for the mess we have made.

Endnotes

1. Angela Merkel speech to CDU youth conference in Potsdam, October 16, 2010.
2. WWF "Living Planet Report," October 2010.
3. Peak Oil: Implications of Resource Scarcity on Security, Zentrum für Transformation der Bundeswehr, Department of Future Studies July 2010.

PART 4

LIGHT IN AN AGE OF "ENDARKENMENT"

The last section of this book examines how we can respond to the problems we have created, the financial and resource demands, as well as the social challenges. Chapter thirteen looks at the simple changes we can make, and some reasonably easy options that will reduce the chance of us having to face a more difficult future than we otherwise might.

Chapter fourteen looks at some of the more radical options we might consider to avoid getting into a financial mess again, and to ensure that the world's natural resources are better protected for future generations. The ideas in this chapter are more difficult and will be wholly unpalatable to many.

Finally, the last chapter addresses the question of responsibility. Who is responsible for fixing these troubles?

13

WE NEED TO CHANGE

Facts do not cease to exist because they are ignored.

Aldous Huxley

The future we face is bleak. We may not be in line for another dose of the Dark Ages with the attendant disintegration of much civilized society, continuously warring states and frequent famines. But we are certainly heading in that direction. We have financial woes, which we cannot fix without a radical change in thinking. There is a serious resource crunch in the offing, which will affect almost everyone on the planet as well as all future generations. And there are growing threats to stability and social cohesion.

These problems will be resolved, of course. It is how they will be resolved that is the question. Will humankind step up to the challenges that lie ahead and tackle them as one united species? Will we endure the hardships together for the good of our societies and our children?

Or will we trip at the first hurdle and fall? Will we choose instead the path of chaos and self-interest?

We can probably find a way to muddle through the financial troubles and the oil shortages. We can manage the debts, somehow. And there are a dozen possible replacements for oil, although we will probably need to use them all. To resolve both of these challenges, however, will be expensive, messy and complicated. There will be many pitfalls along the way and bountiful opportunities for fractious conflicts between nations to develop.

We can also change our diets. For millions of us there is little risk of famine, poorer health or shorter lives. But for hundreds of millions there is.

Much thought will need to be given to dreams and expectations too. Some countries and billions of people will need to lower their expectations—and substantially. They will have to accept that the living standard their children can expect will be no better than theirs, and it may be worse. Many developing countries will also have to accept that they will never become industrialized nations as they once hoped. Places such as China and India will have to accept that the majority of their citizens will never achieve the standard of living common in the West today. The resources are simply not there.

We can stop having so many children. We can create a world that makes fewer demands on the earth's natural resources, not more.

We may find diplomatic answers to the sources of conflict between the world's peoples. Calm talking can remove the need for guns, home-made spears and missiles.

It is comforting to think that this is what will happen, at least for now. It is better to see that sort of future than anything more bleak, which would only induce insomnia. We hope there will be a transition, a muddling through, and that it will all right. That it will not change our lives very much.

But it will. Even without war and widespread famine, billions of us will have to modify what we do, cut the resources we use, and change what we value. We will have to change our lives, whether we want to or not.

Those who embrace the changes will find them hard. It will require a different way of thinking from today, a new way of seeing the world and our relation to it. For those who resist the changes, however, and that is likely to be the majority, the transformation will be tougher still.

Such resistance will add even further to the perils ahead.

You Just Need a New Washer, Mate

There are many wise people, even some award-winning economists working in Washington, who think that the West's financial problems can be repaired easily. They see simple fixes. All we need to do is make a few changes in some places and these troubles will be gone. The engine is just faltering. A new washer, a bit more fuel and a tug on the right levers and it will be fixed in no time.

Their solutions are certainly tantalizing. They say that all we need to do is act together to coordinate a global policy to pull us out of the debt spiral. If we can boost spending in countries where there is still the capacity to consume, and liberalize those with stifling restrictions, new opportunities will be unleashed and the world will soon be back on the road to growth, they say.

The trouble with these ideas is that these economists see the problem as the solution. They demand more spending, more consumption and an even wider adoption of modern, free-market economic ideas. Some of the proponents acknowledge the problems this approach has created, the imbalances and over-use of resources, but they argue that these can be fixed. When the economy is back in balance, they say, we will have the time to think about how to fill in the cracks. We can rely on humankind's enduring ability to innovate, they say, without understanding that there are laws of nature that need to be overcome.

While their suggestions seem attractive, they are unlikely to work. When times are economically difficult, countries do not act together for the common good for long. The G-20 countries were willing to come together in 2008 to stabilize the financial system at the peak of the crisis. But by the end of 2010 they were in disarray again, more interested in their own objectives than any global fix. Moreover, what these economists propose is unfair. It suggests that countries that have been frugal need to take a hit on their savings, just to reduce the debt mountain facing those that overspent.

The solutions proposed are also wrong. Encouraging the citizens of spendthrift countries to consume more is only going to bring them the same troubles that have beset the US—too much debt, no savings, and societies focused on material gain. To cajole China into becoming a consumer-driven society laden with debt too, just to fix the problems in many Western countries, makes no sense. Nor is it possible. There are not enough natural resources on the planet for China to spend its way into Western oblivion.

It is as if these economists want to impose a failed US-centric model on the rest of the world—one based on unrestricted markets, consumerism and profit—in the hope that its universal application will fix the system's obvious flaws. Such foolishness will only make the long-term outlook worse. The world's debt balloon needs to be reduced, not expanded. We need to consume less, not more.

Instead, the economic ideas used in the West need to change, returning to something more like Smith originally intended. We need to implement changes that are equal in magnitude to the scale of the problems we face. This means we need to make fundamental adjustments to our social philosophies.

1. Western economies need to shrink back

We will have to bite the bullet. Much of the West and Japan need to dispense with their stimulus packages and plan, instead, for government cutbacks, reduced consumer spending, and tax hikes. Economies need to be pruned back until they are viable.

To solve the debt problems, most countries in the West, as well as Japan and Australia, need structural economic change. Their governments need to introduce policies that are sustainable and repair the damage caused in the last thirty years. In the public sector there needs to be permanent cuts in state spending and much higher rates of taxation.

The impact of such changes will be massive and difficult. Even then there is no guarantee they will work and some governments will still face default. But they are the only practical steps we can take to address the enormous debt. Additionally, consumers in most of the affected countries (Japan is an exception) need to be forced to save more and spend less. They need to be persuaded to think about the long term.

The level of government spending cuts necessary varies from country to country. In the US, UK, Japan, Greece, Ireland, Spain and many other countries, the cuts will have to be painfully deep and prolonged. In other places such as Germany they need not be so drastic. But in almost all places, state and personal budgets need to be brought back into balance. This is the only way the debt burden can be reduced without risking economic collapse.

In most of these countries, cutbacks of the scale needed will have structural consequences for other parts of the world. Higher taxes, lower government spending and less free-spending consumers will force many indebted economies to shrink. As a result, factories in China, and mines in Africa, places geared to supply developed markets with goods, either directly or indirectly, will face difficult challenges too.

Implementing such cuts will be hard, because they will have to be deep and last long. Already the UK is planning cuts that will be maintained until 2015. The US has a debt problem that will continue to grow until at least 2019. So the cuts there will need to be more prolonged still.

To be successful, there will need to be a change in attitude on the part of almost everyone involved. Here, at least so far, the response of trade unions in the UK, Greece and France is discouraging. The function of unions is to establish and protect the rights of workers. It is not to defend a broken financial system just to maintain jobs or retirement ages. The unions need to understand that there is a wider problem that needs to be addressed. They have a vital role to play, informing their members about the need for fundamental economic change.

There needs to be a substantial change in the attitudes of business managers and citizens too. This will inevitably take time and there will be many false dawns along the way. It is natural for those affected to resist difficult change. Yet quick fixes risk the creation of yet more unsustainable bubbles. Many in the West need to realize—and accept—that the level of economic activity of the past was neither normal, nor sustainable. It was a debt-fueled bubble, a freak of economics, which had consequences.

The result of these cuts, the new normal, will be much lower volumes of economic activity. The challenge for those in charge will be in navigating a route to this lower level of activity without generating chaos along the way. Western consumers will have to realize that they cannot continue to spend anything like the amounts they once did.

Cuts of the scale needed will also change the nature of Western consumer demand. The new austerity will bring a reappearance of the mentality that makes people repair, make-do and mend—to live more sustainably, as well as more frugally. Western consumers will demand products that last longer and that use the world's resources better. Laundromats and car-sharing businesses, as well as companies that allow people to borrow everything from fancy handbags to garden tools and bicycles, are the sort that need to prosper.

Conventional businesses, however, will suffer. They face declining sales volumes, a drop in the prices they can achieve, and a fall in their share prices. Finding investors for such companies will be tough. They will also face much higher taxes.

Raising almost all forms of taxation will be necessary too. The easiest taxes to raise are probably those levied on businesses, as well as fuel, inheritance and capital gains, which have been mostly low for many years. Increasing these taxes should also be easier than putting up income or sales tax.

The tax on fuel will need to rise not just for environmental reasons, but because governments will need to raise money and cut their oil imports. This is especially true in the US. Countries that currently subsidize fuel prices, including India, China, Russia and Iran, will have to reduce such incentives gradually in the interests of protecting reserves.

Taxing the dead is also easier than taxing the living. They are less troublesome, even if their offspring complain. With governments confronting such large debts the dead can provide a rich seam of necessary funds.

Similarly, taxes on capital gains made through investments—be it in shares or houses—will need to rise sharply too. This will have the added benefit of punishing the finance sector, which many taxpayers feel has been the cause of the debt. It will also make it harder for banks to grow too large, reducing another source of economic instability. Taxing property gains will make home buyers understand that their houses are not a source of income. They are places to live.

Legislators will also need to raise retirement ages. The age at which people are forced to work will have to rise in many professions to well beyond seventy years old.

In the US, of course, the notion of such changes will be especially hard to accept. They are alien to American principles. It will take a long time for legislators to accept the need for radical government spending cuts and tax rises, because it runs against the American way of life.

Taking the necessary steps will be made even harder by the "fruitcakes" in the Tea Party, who seem to think that the solution to America's problems comes from less government, or none at all. While such ideas may be laudable, they do not address the problem. America cannot repay its massive debts or meet its obligations by cutting government. Americans cannot be made to use the world's oil reserves more responsibly by means of persuasion. The responsibility to pay pensions to state employees, finance the losses of Fannie and Freddie and pay off the government's existing debt obligations will remain, no matter how small they make the government in Washington. Even armed insurrection, already talked about by some in the Tea Party, and apparently with some seriousness, will not release America from its debt burden or its obligations to the rest of humanity. Although it might take a decade before those in power in America come around to the idea, the US is going to have to change if the world is to address its challenges. The American economy is going to have to shrink, and the government is going to have to tax much more. Americans are going to have to use fewer natural resources. Either that, or America will have to default on its debts and obligations, bringing chaos to us all.

2. *We need to price the world's resources properly*

Responding to the environmental problems and troubles caused by over-use of the world's resources will also need tougher laws and higher taxes. Just as with many of the debts, most of the environmental and resource problems have been caused by under-pricing and a lack of sufficient legislation. Where adequate laws exist, they have often been poorly enforced.

The most obvious way to reduce the volume of resources we use is to put up the price. And the best way to achieve that is through resolutely applied taxation and legislative control. This has the added benefit of encouraging better use of the resources we have left. It will also give people an incentive to innovate. In the energy market, for example, much progress could be achieved by using our remaining oil more efficiently. Those responsible for getting the stuff out the ground and designing engines would quickly find ways to use it more efficiently if the price was significantly higher than today. Higher prices will also change consumer behavior, forcing people to take fewer trips, and repair, rather than replace, the items they own.

Similarly, the most obvious way to discontinue the practices of those who pollute, over-fish or damage the environment in any way, is to penalize these activities—and heavily enough that they will stop. Forcing polluting firms to close, confiscating the boats of greedy fishermen, and impounding the homes and assets of those who finance logging, would concentrate their minds.

The trouble is how to implement such ideas globally and how to manage the effects. As the price of many items would rise, such measures would penalize the poor more than the rich. There is also a risk that the governments of many developing nations would see such laws as unfair, limiting their right or ability to industrialize, or develop economically. Such hurdles, however, should not stop us trying.

Another option is simply to tax raw material use, activities causing wild fish stock depletion, and products derived from rainforest destruction, very heavily. Taxes would need to be high enough to put a price on the externalities, the costs of using these resources that we currently ignore. Announcing, for example, that in ten years time a barrel of oil will cost twenty times what it does today—about $3,000 a barrel—would give the world time and a powerful incentive to develop alternatives. It would give a clear signal too, that we have ten years to change the way we live. The price would need to rise steadily throughout that time, to ramp up the effect.

Such a change would make us realize that we have to become less dependent on cars and aircraft for personal transportation and prepare for that. We could also tax other sources of waste, and factors that contribute to ill health, at the same time. We can penalize manufacturers of fatty foods and those using transfats. This would reduce medical costs and make people healthier, allowing them to live better lives. We can also tax packaging businesses, to reduce waste and unnecessary resource use there.

Similar taxes could be levied on products that use other resources that are in need of protection, either in the countries where they are extracted, in the countries where they are transformed into finished goods, or where they are used. To be effective, countries unwilling to comply would need to be subject to heavy sanctions, to penalize their unfair use of the world's remaining resources—because the world's remaining resources actually belong to us all, equally. Of course, the prices for many goods would rise sharply. But that is only right. We have been paying too little for decades.

Similarly, any product which contains ingredients such as palm oil, rubber, or any other product grown on land where rainforests once stood, could be taxed in such a way as to make the further clearance of rainforests wholly uneconomic. These taxes could be applied on the end-user. Trade in wood from many trees could be banned, as is the case with ivory and some animal parts today. Even trade in any existing products made from these woods could be banned or very tightly controlled.

In the same way, fishing from unsustainable sources, and the use of bear paws, tiger parts and tusks, could be universally banned—with heavy policing of countries that try to circumvent the regulations. Loopholes, such as those used by Japan to continue whaling where it is unsustainable for what it euphemistically calls "research purposes," would need to be closed. Again, penalties for non-compliance will need to be severe.

Raising taxes like this would obviously increase the costs of almost everything we buy, making life tougher for millions. But at least the taxes raised would have another benefit, beyond changing the way we value the world's resources. They would help pay off some of the world's debts.

Such ideas would undoubtedly be very difficult to apply. But that is the challenge we face. Not addressing the problems will not make them go away. We will eventually face a world without fish, rainforests and oil, unless we act. If we are to be successful, we have to implement unpalatable measures and enforce them.

Doing nothing is not a responsible option. It will only make the problems worse.

3. Profits need to be "fair," businesses need to meet society's needs

If we are to overcome the problems we face we will also need to redesign the West's approach to business, and adopt different objectives and measures of success.

We will need to rethink the role of banks and companies in society. Since 2008 many plans for changing bank regulations have been recommended but almost all have been reactive and piecemeal: they have sought to restrict the activities of financial services companies, but they have struggled against the strong resistance of bankers and the fact that financial services companies have the freedom to relocate, or the means to circumvent many of the demands of legislators who are able to make laws that can be applied domestically or regionally.

We need to approach the issue more fundamentally, to redesign the business side of our economic systems from its foundations.

One way we might start thinking about this is by looking at the profits that businesses make. In classical economics, "normal" profits are defined as returns that are sufficient to keep someone in business, long term. The word "sufficient" is critical. Economics was originally under-pinned by the important notion of fairness. Profits should always be reasonable. If they were not, goes the theory, competition will bring them back into line. This process has not been functioning, in the finance business and many other sectors too.

Smith wrote about how important it was to maintain the "laws of justice" in economics, about the need for efficiency and sustainability. He believed that economic wealth should not just benefit individuals, but wider society too. To be in harmony, an economic system should offer "natural recompense" for work, he said. Smith warned that when profits were too high, ruin would soon follow, just as it has today.

> The rate of profit . . . is naturally low in rich, and high in poor countries, and it is always highest in the countries which are going fastest to ruin.
>
> ADAM SMITH[1]

Modern economic concepts of business in the West are not supported by such ideas. They are not in harmony. Indeed, the opposite has been the case during the last thirty years—businesses in rich countries have generated the highest profits. The classical system has not been working.

We need to return to the ideas of classical economics and think about the value of businesses to society. Businesses exist to make a profit and they should be free to behave as they wish, or at least mostly free. But they also have a responsibility to society. They should not be allowed to make excessive profits long term or act against the needs of society, by increasing income inequality or selling goods that make us ill, for example.

A comparison between Volkswagen and Goldman Sachs helps illustrate the point.

In 2009, Volkswagen had sales of $137 billion. From this, it made a profit of $1.2 billion, which is not a very large return for this sort of sales volume: less than 1 percent. The car business is a tough one. Even so, Volkswagen shows in its accounts that it generated an added value to the world of almost $29 billion. This is what it contributed to society. Most of this was generated through employment. Some was given as dividends to investors and some was given to the state, in the form of taxes. Volkswagen employed 368,500 people that year and made a profit of $3,256 per person. This is surely a "reasonable" return by any measure, given how much value the company brings to society.

Of course, this does not cover all the externality costs that Volkswagen brings to society. Volkswagen does not pay for the pollution caused by the use of its vehicles and in the manufacturing process. There is no cost allocated for the congestion or road deaths that result from the use of its cars. Nor does Volkswagen pay the full costs of the environmental damage caused by the extraction of the raw materials needed to make its vehicles, or the full costs incurred during their disposal.

Modern economics still needs to find a way to do that.

Even so, by any reasonable standard, Volkswagen is contributing positively to society. It is making products people want, it is employing hundreds of thousands of people, and it is making fair returns, enough to invest in its future.

The same cannot be said for many of the financial institutions that have made the Western economic world so unstable. Nor can the same be said for those who have made their profits from simply buying and selling items, without adding any value. It cannot be said for those buying and selling houses, commodities and companies.

These people have mostly made money without any economic or social added value at all. They have simply bought low, encouraged or waited for the market to rise, and then sold when the price is high. They have done nothing of economic value, but they have become rich.

During 2009, Goldman Sachs made a profit of $13.4 billion or $422,700 per employee. In the first three months, when the bank was in receipt of $10 billion of US government aid, it still made more profit than Volkswagen did in the entire year.

Almost all of Goldman's profits came from the trading division. Some were generated as a result of the US government bailout of other financial institutions, such as AIG. During much of 2009, Goldman made a profit of more than $100 million a day, gambling on the market. Like so many other banks, Goldman had been allowed to generate revenues through gambling—but with the ability to fiddle the outcome in its favor. This is the bank that its boss, Lloyd Blankfein, believes is "doing God's work," but which *Rolling Stone* magazine described as "a great vampire squid wrapped around the face of humanity, relentlessly jamming its blood funnel into anything that smells like money."

In redesigning the economic system we need to ask ourselves some fundamental questions. What do we want our banks and businesses to do? Is it fair for a bank to make ten times the profit of a car manufacturer when that excess return comes not from supporting economic growth, or financing business development, but from gambling? Is it fair that a food company can sell products that make us fat and unhealthy, when society as a whole has to pick up the medical costs that result? Are these the sorts of businesses we want to encourage or restrict?

4. *Markets need Goldilocks management*

Behind this we need to think about the role and purpose of markets and governments too. We need to ensure that our societies, and the way they are run, are sustainable and just. Market economics and governments have a vital role to play in achieving this. But both should meet society's needs to provide as many people as possible with a full and healthy life. Of course it is impossible to create a system to do this perfectly. But we know we can achieve a greater degree of fairness than in the last thirty years.

Markets should not be left entirely free. We should run them, not have them run us. They should operate according to Enlightenment principles of openness as well as fairness. They need to operate within a framework of rules, which are established and enforced by democratically elected governments. They should not be unregulated or under-regulated because they need to serve the needs of people, of society. They should not be manipulated or controlled by a few for their own gain, or be allowed to damage lives. They should not act against the interests of society. It was the lack of proper regulation in the US, UK, and many other places, which caused most of the problems the world has today. But they should not be over-regulated either, as they are in state-controlled economies.

Is it possible for markets to be "Goldilocks" regulated—not too much and not too little, but just the right amount? They can. And Germany's *Ordnungspolitik* offers an example from one of the most successful, strong and stable economies in the world in the last fifty years.

There is no easy or direct translation of *Ordnungspolitik*, although it roughly means something like "the policies needed to keep the system in balance." Originally developed after the Great Crash, it is a political and economic philosophy designed to control both the market and the state. It is a system used in other European countries too, although often with modifications.

Smith would have applauded the philosophy because *Ordnungspolitik* strives to guarantee competition and the economic freedom of the individual. It separates the state from the market as much as possible, so that the state is only given the power to intervene when markets do not function properly. This intervention could be when there is a need for public goods—such as schools, defense or power infrastructure; when there are natural monopolies—such as in the provision of water, gas or electricity; or when cartels have been formed by private companies that are anticompetitive.

What makes *Ordnungspolitik* different from many other Western systems, notably those in the US and UK, is that the state also has a duty to change market results when they are in conflict with social policy, economic efficiency and growth. This means, for example, that if the government sees growing income disparities, too much wealth flowing to too few people, it has a duty to intervene and bring the system back into *Ordnung*, into balance. The system recognizes that over-regulation is to be avoided because it weakens the market mechanism. But it also recognizes that markets left to their own devices sometimes act against the interests of society.

There are seven basic principles:[2]

1. There needs to be a functioning price mechanism. Government policies should avoid all measures that distort prices through subsidies, tariffs or non-tariff barriers, trade barriers, cartels and monopolies.
2. There should be a stable monetary system. Governments should seek to achieve price stability through monetary policy.
3. Markets should be open and trade free. Governments should avoid regulations that inhibit open or free competition, but they should stop the creation of monopolies and cartels.
4. The rights of property and private ownership should be protected, because they act as an incentive for market participants.
5. There must be freedom of contract to ensure fair competition. That is, individuals and companies are free to form contracts with whomever they wish, so long as they do not impede the freedom of the market—through the creation of a cartel, for example.
6. Market participants must be held accountable for any liabilities they incur through contractual agreements. Those who make mistakes or bad decisions are responsible for them.
7. Economic policies should ensure stability, to develop trust. Stability reduces risk in decision making for entrepreneurs, investors, and consumers. Bubbles are to be avoided.

These principles are not perfect, and Germany has itself occasionally violated them: many of its banks were also badly caught out when they lent too much during the US housing boom.

But they set a framework to control the market only where it needs to be controlled. Germany and Austria also try to ensure that there is a fair distribution of wealth[3] in their societies. The system is designed to encourage fairness, to make sure that it functions for the good of society. The American and British systems are, by their nature, much more divisive. This makes them more unstable too, allowing bubbles to form and encouraging a polarized society of haves and have nots. *Ordnungspolitik* is an attempt to address the failings of this under-regulated, free-market system.

Ordnungspolitik offers a middle road between the two extremist political ideologies of the twentieth century—capitalism and communism. Both failed because they lead to a concentration of power in distant and unaccountable institutions. In the communist system, power became too concentrated in government, in the hands of a few. In the free-market system, power became too concentrated in the private sector, in the hands of a small number of people running big companies and banks.

The under-regulated, free-market model, allowed us to create a world where many of the biggest economic powers were not countries or governments at all. They were finance companies and businesses. Because they were not being regulated properly, these firms were largely unaccountable to society. Few of the world's largest corporations or banks had any serious social objectives at all, yet they managed much of the economies, and so the societies, in which they operated. They existed with the sole purpose of making a profit. That is not a market economy the way Smith ever intended it, despite the calls of industrialists and politicians in the US for less "red tape" and less regulation.

Many of those living in the West have been fooled into thinking that a benefit of their economic freedom was the growth of these monolithic corporations. They believed that such banks and businesses reflected the power of the market, the underlying strength it has to grow, and create wealth unaided.

But these businesses and banks are actually centrally planned institutions, just like the government ministries of communist states. Their managers decide where jobs are made or lost, and the industries that should receive investment without recourse to society, just as in a centrally planned economy. The bosses of big business decide what is going to happen in much of the world, not the elected representatives of the people. They decide to pollute rivers in China to make cheap toys for children in Chicago, regardless of what that means for the citizens of China, or for jobs in America.

They externalize the costs.

Despite the mantra of the last thirty years, markets need governments. Regulators need to ensure that costs are fully internalized—that the costs to the environment are fully priced into what we buy. The success of many economies after World War II was not down to unregulated free-markets, it was down to having markets that functioned in a strong regulatory framework set by democratically accountable governments.

We need to go back to that.

Endnotes

1. Adam Smith, *An Inquiry into the Nature and Causes of the Wealth of Nations* (London: W. Strahan and T. Cadell, 1776), bk.1, ch.11, conclusion.
2. *Grundprinzipien der Wirtschaftspolitik*, Walter Eucken, 1952. Also "Miracles are Possible," or "A Classic German Approach to the Current Crisis," Tim H. Stuchtey, *AICGS Transatlantic Perspectives*, Johns Hopkins University, June 2009.
3. Prof. Klaus Dieter John, "The German Social Market Economy—(Still) a Model for the European Union?" *Theoretical and Applied Economics* (Germany: Professor Chemnitz Technical University, 2007), vol. 3(508), issue 3(508), pages 3–10.

14

OTHER OPTIONS NEED DEBATE

For every complex problem there is a simple solution that is wrong.

George Bernard Shaw

From Progress to Poverty

The more radical options that are open to us are, perhaps inevitably, harder to conceptualize and implement. Many ideas that could address the world's problems sound appealing but do not work, either because they have consequences we do not want, or because they are impractical. Radical proposals are also likely to face more resistance when we try to implement them. People do not like big changes, especially those who benefit from the *status quo,* no matter what the benefits for their children might be.

Niccolò Machiavelli was right when he said:

> There is nothing more difficult to execute than to introduce a new order to things; for he who introduces it has all those who profit from the old order as his enemies; and he has only lukewarm allies in all those who might profit from the new. This lukewarmness partly stems from fear and partly from the skepticism of men, who do not truly believe in new things unless they have personal experience in them.

Yet humanity needs to ask itself some fundamental questions, which have not been asked for a very long time.

- Is it right for anyone to profit from the exploitation of the world's resources if, through these actions, others in this or future generations are harmed?
- How can we make sure that everything given in nature is for the equal benefit of all humanity?
- As the most intelligent form of life, do we have a responsibility to protect diversity in nature and the sustainable survival of other species?
- What should humankind's objectives be and how should we measure progress?
- Should we stop anyone making a profit from a business that has no social value?
- How can we ensure that no one suffers from the economic activities of others?
- How should we provide charity, welfare, equality of opportunity and the greatest possible benefit to the greatest number of people while protecting the world for future generations?

Give the Flowers the Power

It is not necessary to be a hippy, hugging trees and living in a VW campervan, to see that something is wrong with the way we value our world. It does not take much thought to see that the under-regulated *laissez-faire* model of economics and the politics of the free market are to blame for many of our excesses. While it may not seem like it very often, we need to remember that we have a choice. We can choose to get off the path that only seeks economic growth for its own sake, which requires mass consumerism, and which is measured mostly by monetary gain. There are steps we can take to protect the world's natural resources for future generations—as long as we are willing to behave differently.

Classical economics says that development and prosperity require four elements—land, labor, capital and enterprise. It says we need resources, the honest toil of effort, finance and someone with the gumption to bring these elements together to produce something. The reward for this is profit. When profits are too high, competitors emerge, driving down the returns until they are "normal," according to the theory.

In each element there is a need for responsibility and balance. Labor should not be exploited, capital needs to behave responsibly, and entrepreneurs have a duty to society. Similarly, land is not just a resource for us to use without consequence. Our consumption of it has to be sustainable. We have to manage the human scale of economic activities so as not to disrupt nature, certainly to the extent that we risk destroying it. That would be suicidal. That cannot be the objective of any rational sort of economic system.

Modern economics has not achieved this. It has not managed the scale of our activities or encouraged responsible use. It has allowed us to exploit nature, regardless of the consequences. It has provided us with a model that encourages us to destroy large swathes of the planet in the interests of short-term profit. This model *is* suicidal.

To avoid making this destruction worse, we need to abandon many modern economic ideas. We need to consider, instead, concepts that will feel odd, like putting on the clothes of our ancestors. One option, for example, may be to implement the ideas of US political economist Henry George. Although his suggestions were particularly popular at the end of the nineteenth century, his concepts echo those of enlightenment thinkers such as David Ricardo and Mill.

1. Our remaining resources should be protected for everyone

George's ideas are simple, but still seem radical today. He said that everything found in nature—land and the world's resources—belongs to humankind. To stop anyone profiting from these resources, the gains from nature should be taxed, he said. Taxing these profits allows the benefits of nature to be evenly distributed. It ensures that the world's resources are not exploited for individual or corporate gain. He assumed, of course, that governments were competent and able to do this.

George saw then, as now, that there was a massively unequal distribution of wealth in society. Too much of the wealth was going to land-owners and monopolists, just as now. In the nineteenth century the wealth was being taken by the robber-barons of the oil and rail industries. Today, it is the executives running the IT, oil and banking industries, which are making profits and incomes far in excess of their needs. George saw inequality as an injustice that caused poverty for millions. He believed that it should be corrected through taxation.

We could adopt these ideas today. We could effectively nationalize the world's resources, making them the property of governments, or some global authority. A first step could be in taxing the profits of resource-extracting companies—such as those in the mining sector, oil and gas—at 100 percent. This would ensure that the world's resources were immediately better protected, and their benefits could be allocated more fairly. Of course, companies would not get into the resources business if all their earnings were confiscated. So these companies would need to be taken under state control in some way too. It would then be up to individual states or some international authority to work out how to extract and use the world's resources and distribute the revenue generated. It would mean that miners and oil company engineers would work for governments, which would then decide how to use what nature has given.

Taxing natural resources and taking them into public ownership like this may be impossible, of course, although some countries have already managed it. The biggest concern is the competence of the legislators to manage what they would then control. But that is a secondary issue. The primary issue is to ensure that the world's resources are used to meet the needs of all of us, that they are not extracted by companies for profit. Controlling oil and gas reserves, as well as other raw materials, would also allow governments to price them correctly, accounting for the externalities.

Even if George's ideas only help us to think differently, they can achieve much along the way.

Similarly, if we controlled water rights better, then farmers could be encouraged to save more water and grow less water-intensive crops. This would reduce the need for dams and expensive irrigation systems. Land, which is controlled by rich farmers and used wastefully, for cattle, for example, could be used more efficiently and equitably. Properly applied, taxes or legislation can be used to change the way huge swathes of land are used. Laws can provide the poor with greater access to land that is presently underused, for example. This would also discourage them from trying to farm wetlands, wildlife reserves, or destroy rainforests to create additional land for farming.

Such ideas would change the way everyone thinks about how the world's resources are used. People need to become more aware of waste and of their damaging behavior. The world's resources need to become a priority for all of us.

2. Undeserved gains should be fully taxed on ethical grounds

George went further in his book, *Progress and Poverty,* saying that any profits made from land and property should be regarded as immoral. They should also be taxed for ethical reasons, because any profit made this way is unearned, and so undeserved. The gain belongs to the entire community. Unless such gains are taxed, he said, the price of land increases as populations grow. This means that later generations have to pay more for their land, making future generations poorer. As a result, George believed that land-ownership was a *cause* of poverty. To George, like Smith, equality was vital. Ensuring that no one could profit from land was an essential element of a meritocratic society.

Such ideas are much more eye-brow raising today than they were in the nineteenth century, reflecting how far our thinking has shifted. Some of George's ideas were included in the UK Liberal Party's manifesto of 1909, and the town of Fairhope in Alabama was founded to test his theories.

That Pip Squeak?

The implications of applying such ideas today would be radical. Many people have made a lot of money out of speculation, especially in property. Why should society not tax their unearned gains? They have not done anything of value to achieve their wealth, they have simply speculated on the price of land. Their wealth could provide much needed funds to rebalance many national accounts. In the same way, the profits made by banks in their dealing operations, or by investors who buy and sell shares for short-term gain, would be confiscated too, taken by the state to repair the damage such activities have wrought. Private equity companies and hedge funds that strip businesses for profit, leaving them unable to survive long term, could be included too. Similarly, instigating a 100 percent death tax to stop attempts to transfer wealth between generations, would ensure we all start from the same place. It would be meritocratic.

Such taxation of unearned wealth, however, would not apply to those who were genuine investors, to those who put wealth into a business for months or years. Such investors would be allowed a "fair" return for the risk they have taken before they were taxed. This might be equivalent to the prevailing rate of interest, plus a percentage for risk. But for speculators, for traders buying and selling stocks, currencies or other items, there should be no such reward. The only risk they face is that the price of what they buy and sell rises or falls because the market shifts, perhaps because of other speculators. Ethical taxes would eradicate these gains to bring a halt to businesses that serve no social purpose and offer no value.

3. Economic growth should be regarded as a happy consequence not a purpose

We also need to rethink the concept of progress. Western economies have become obsessed with growth for its own sake. Social progress during the last thirty years has been measured by how much economies grow, in monetary terms. How much they grow has depended almost entirely on how much Western societies consume. We have reached an odd place: without increasing consumption there is no growth—and without growth, there is no progress.

All this is wrong-headed, focused on a pointless goal. It stems from the warped economic ideas of the last few decades. For much of the last few hundred years businesses and economies did not grow much at all. Businesses made steady incomes each year, paid employees much the same, and provided a purpose for those involved. There was progress, but of a different sort. Societies had other values, not based on shopping and consumption. Family, philanthropy, exploration, science and discovery were more important—although, so was the conquest of foreign lands at times.

In *One Life at a Time Please*, published in 1988, Edward Abbey an American author and environmentalist, wrote, "[w]e can see that the religion of endless growth—like any religion based on blind faith rather than reason—is a kind of mania, a form of lunacy, indeed a disease. Growth for the sake of growth is the ideology of the cancer cell."[1]

Our obsession with growth means we have forgotten many of the original principles of the Enlightenment. We push ever harder to achieve efficiency, but sacrifice fairness along the way. People are made redundant just to improve short-term profits. Some western governments are obsessed with lowering taxes, to the extent that millions suffer. In the US this has led to a country where tens of millions are denied healthcare, much of the infrastructure is decaying, libraries have been closed and schools can barely function. Citizens have been abandoned, left with the hope that the free market will somehow fix these problems. They are expected to believe that free enterprise will magically attract businesses and provide jobs where they live. With the jobs come healthcare and security. But without educated people to employ, or a decent place to live, the businesses go elsewhere.

Worse, in most of the Western world, progress is not just dependent on consumption. It has become steadily more dependent on debt too. People work to live, and live to consume. Society has become based on greed. Western citizens are encouraged to maximize their own gains. Businesses are told to maximize their profits—not in the long term, as classical economics says, but in the short term, to feed the growth engine further. Through the magic of the market, we are told that this will lead to a general rise in overall wealth and lead to social progress.

Only it hasn't.

Modern economics has twisted the ideas of classical economists. Economics was a subject that originally stemmed from moral philosophy. Its theories were based on concepts of equality, fairness and value, not undeserved profit and selfishness. Smith abhorred lobbyists, or special interest groups, seeking to distort the market or twist the minds of legislators for their own gain. He believed that governments needed to control the market to stop abuses and constrain the tendency of companies to monopolize their businesses. He believed the rich should pay much higher taxes than the poor, particularly on their properties. He said the rich should pay a disproportionately higher share of taxes because they were able to. Maximizing short-term gains without constraint, as we do today in much of the world, is not classical economics.

Mill also believed strongly in the rights of individuals to act as they wish. We interpret this today as a nod to selfishness. Yet Mill was very clear. An individual acting alone needs to be constrained if such actions harm others.

Such thinking has been lost today. In Mill's day, irresponsible lending by banks would have been constrained because it leads to bubbles and financial crises, which bring unemployment and poverty. They create harm. Similarly, if consuming a country's water or coal resources brings poverty to that country, or limits the chances of it developing in the future, it needs to be stopped. Exploiting African nations' resources to the detriment of their societies is not classical economics.

Mill's concept of harm also affects how we behave in other ways. If we see a child running into the street and fail to help, we are causing harm because we are not acting responsibly or compassionately for others. If we avoid paying taxes, we are not playing our part in society. If unfettered accumulation of wealth means we ruin the environment and reduce the overall quality of life, it is better for the economy to stagnate.

This is not complicated. With freedom, as well as power, comes responsibility.

When we think about what we want from our economies and societies, we could do worse than look again at Smith's early ideas, at what he called *The Theory of Moral Sentiments*. Smith strongly believed in notions of compassion, benevolence and a sense of propriety. Men and women need to have respect for each other and be judged by their actions. Too often, today's financiers have escaped the effects of their actions—the poverty their lending has caused. They have not treated society with respect; quite the opposite. George believed that human institutions need to conform to natural principles. He saw that nature favored symbiosis. Our ideas and social philosophies need to be in balance with nature.

Smith believed that well-functioning societies are not the result of good government. He believed that we all need to act with self-control. Society needs to be driven through generosity and humanity, not anger or the "selfish passions" of grief and joy. Joy stimulates envy in others, he said, so modesty is prudent. People should proceed in gradual steps—instant wealth or massive progress in a short time can never be deserved, he said.

A vital question we need to think about is whether or not we can achieve economic growth without using more of the world's resources, without creating further pollution and waste. We need to think about why we want growth. Growth creates economic wealth but it also creates pollution and inequality. Can we generate the wealth without the problems that it brings? Ecological economists believe not. They regard the increased scale of human activity as the cause of environmentally damaging activity. They support a steady-state model, without increases in materials and energy consumption, but with increases in services and the quality of goods.

Some countries in Europe have managed to achieve declining rates of energy use and still grow. It is also clear that in most of the world much higher rates of energy efficiency can be achieved. So it may be possible to continue to grow and to reduce resource use simultaneously. At some point though, even this will not be enough. At some point, all the world's resources will be gone and future generations will not be able to sustain themselves.

The usual response to this is to suggest that technology and human ingenuity will provide a solution. We will learn to generate energy from other sources such as hydrogen. But we are not able to recreate many other chemicals and resources, so this argument only goes so far. We cannot replicate copper, uranium and zinc. The laws of chemistry make it impossible for us to reconstitute many of the elements that are vital to us after they have been changed. We cannot recreate the world's hydrocarbons when they have been burnt, nor the coral reefs or rainforests when they have been destroyed. Ingenuity can only take us so far.

More importantly, simply hoping that we will find a solution is not responsible, given the scale and nature of the problem. It would be to adopt the behavior of the dinosaurs noticing an impending Ice Age and hoping it will soon get warmer. It is morally indefensible for us to use up most of the world's resources in a few generations without rationing them, or taking any responsibility for the consequences. We have a duty to our grandchildren.

We do not think about the consequences because we are driven by the need for economic growth. We worry that responsible use of the world's resources will lead to stagnation and unemployment. So we ignore the problem we are creating. Yet, morally, we need to find a way to live with low growth or no growth at all.

4. *We need to rethink the role of philanthropy and charity*

There is also something out of alignment in the way our world provides charity, either through NGOs, or philanthropic deeds. It is a measure of how much our values have become warped, so that the provision of economic services in this way has grown explosively and now NGOs provide support to innumerable causes.

At first glance, charity seems to be a good thing. Yet NGOs and philanthropic groups are a reflection of a fundamental problem. Charity is an attempt to patch the parts of the system that are not working. Mostly such attempts are well intended. But sometimes they are driven by less enlightened motives. And in almost every case they are a poor way to make up for some of the shortfalls of modern economics. They mop up the externalities—rather than leaving them, like a puddle, for us all to see. Charities actually support many of the warped ideas of social progress by masking them. They have become a substitute for social justice and proper economics.

Charities depend on the desires and incomes of unaccountable donors. Their managers decide where and how the money should be spent. This makes their activities undemocratic too. Governments are subject to regular democratic or political review, as well as public scrutiny and control. The charity business is not. Because of this, the way they spend their money can be subject to favoritism, waste and inefficiency. Just as when a zoo gets visitors to sponsor animals and everyone wants to donate to the tigers, leaving the vast majority of animals unsupported, charity is a way of supporting society's tigers. Donors give more freely to causes that appeal to them, rather than to causes where there may be greater need. Moreover, charities' first loyalties lie with the givers not the receivers, because this ensures a better flow of funds.

As well as having misguided objectives, this means that they can impose conditions on their giving. Money is offered with strings attached. This might be to discourage the use of contraceptives, or to promote American values and the church. More worrying, many of the most polluting industries are also those with the most cash, and because an increasing number of NGOs are competing for a small pool of funds, some charities have even been tempted to become financially dependent on the organizations that are causing many of the problems they say they want to address, undermining their moral foundations.

Charity almost always undermines the freedom of the recipient. It can be unethical too, when it interferes in the self-determination of sovereign states. Charities working in parts of Africa and in places like North Korea, for example, frequently act against the wishes of the state, claiming moral superiority. Their activities can be politically manipulative or even contrary to human rights. Because they have been seen as "doing good," however, these problems are often hidden or ignored.

Similarly, philanthropists rarely fight for social justice. Their actions are founded on an acceptance of injustice. They see their role as trying to mitigate the effects. Today's billionaires do not fight to bring change to the system that created their unequal wealth. Few appear to see any inconsistency or irony in their offering help to the poor. The Gates Foundation attempts to provide greater social inclusion, for example, without attempting to change the system that encourages wider social division.

Corporate social responsibility, the public relations practice that many businesses engage in "to do good," is little better. It takes money that belongs to shareholders and gives it to causes that managers think are worthy, or will improve the company's image in the eyes of consumers and other interested parties.

Enlightenment thinkers were not motivated like this. They had plans to redesign cities, to lift the imagination and ideas of people living there. They built real and metaphorical bridges to a better world. They sought to reform social justice, to bring equal opportunity, and to uplift our species through a new vision for humanity. They fought against the backward influence of religion, encouraging dialogue and openness in the arts, music, literature and the sciences. They sought to encourage the development of an enlightened populace.

Improving the world is not about offering money to seemingly worthy causes. It may be very laudable for Bill Gates and his coterie to try to improve people's lives by offering medicines and encouraging research. It is fine to do good works, providing finance to educate people in less-developed countries, or support bringing water to the poor. It may be useful for California's technology billionaires to give some of their wealth to give to new business start-ups through seed financing.

But sitting in a comfy armchair and handing out financial alms is not what philanthropy should be about. Most of the money being spent promotes Western ideas of progress and development, often explicitly. Moreover, these individuals and their philanthropic organizations alone have decided what is worthy. In the process they make over-population worse, which causes suffering to billions more. Rather than having Gates fund a charity to offer banking to the poor in developing countries using mobile phones, why not encourage the citizens of these places to establish cooperatives, which will allow them to control their own destiny? Then, the profits go back to the community, not some telecoms company or bank.

The efforts of philanthropists may be well-meaning, but they are also often misdirected. Charities frequently fail to understand the issues they are dealing with, or meddle for their own reward. They sometimes even exaggerate the effects of natural disasters such as floods, earthquakes, or droughts because it suits their commercial purposes.

Whether the ideas of philanthropists and charities are right or wrong is not the issue. It is that the decisions are being taken by a handful of wealthy people and some business managers, without them being answerable to society for what they do. Who said Mr Gates and his friends should decide what is best for the world?

Genuine need should not be dependent on handouts at the whim of the rich.

5. We need to rethink how and why we are governed

If the responsibility of governments is to govern, many have abrogated their duties in the last thirty years. They have worshiped at the altar of modern economics and left markets to rule instead.

This suggests that Western ideas of government and democracy need to be revisited. It is not just that regulators have not done what they should have. It is that we have also created a world with a globalized consciousness, but with localized politics. As businesses and banks have become more powerful, regulatory authorities have struggled to know how to manage them.

Without an effective global authority, national governments have become less able to protect the public interest or to force banks and businesses into line. Governments, wherever they are, need to ensure that banks and businesses compete fairly, that they provide secure employment, that they pay a reasonable share of local taxes to provide essential public infrastructure, and that they function as responsible community members.

The logical conclusion is that we need to have global governance to match the influence of global companies. The alternative is to shrink companies to a size which makes them governable—to a scale that allows their excesses to be nationally controlled and ensures the needs of society are met. Alternatively, if we want a market economy that is responsible to society, without having some supra-national authority, we need to change the ownership, structure and management of big businesses to make them locally accountable.

We have created an economy in many countries in which there are just a few suppliers of shampoo, two or three major food retailers, half-a-dozen end-producers of cars and a few big telecoms companies. This would have been anathema to Smith. He was a dedicated foe of large corporations, absentee ownership, trade secrets, and concentrated power. For his economic ideas to work, markets need equality and a distribution of economic power. Equity was not just a matter of justice or fairness to Smith. It was a necessary precondition for protecting the economy and the environment.

Beyond the broader principles, there are other practicalities. In the US, democracy has become badly tarnished. Big business and wealthy individuals provide finance to elect candidates who support their particular ideas. It has become government by the rich, for the rich, even though everyone has the right to vote. Although it is better in many parts of Europe, other countries have seen their democratic ideals undermined in the last thirty years too. Political parties often seem to exist with the sole purpose of being elected to have power. Political reform is minimal, despite the speed of social change. First principles have been forgotten.

We need to think again about what we want government to achieve and where and how we want to be governed. It is tempting to suggest that every citizen should have a say in all the major decisions that affect us. But we are not all heart surgeons. Nor are we all presidents and prime ministers, able to run countries. Adopting the policies of the majority makes us subject to their tyranny. Few people are qualified and dispassionate enough to make decisions about taxation, the death penalty and war, objectively.

But how and where should government be built? National authorities have been badly weakened in their power and influence, by the growth of the private sector, and by the rising mobility of their citizens. Many countries, notably those most badly affected by the financial crisis, only offer two main political parties to choose from. It is as though Goldilocks only had two bowls, one hot and one cold. Many Western citizens, as well as those in China, Japan, and much of the rest of the world, have a wider choice of toilet paper than of political parties.

We need government. We need to have laws and regulations. We need to regulate markets and ensure that society is just. We need elected representatives, supported by a professional bureaucracy, to provide the foundations of modern civilization. In too many places, government has been corrupted and manipulated by a small group of powerful and wealthy individuals. No wonder many people have become disenchanted with mainstream politics. No wonder they find the ideas of those on the fringes increasingly attractive.

We need to find a way to fix this. But how? Arbitrary lines drawn on maps are not a particularly good way to achieve good governance. How we are all governed should not be determined by where we are born. But what are the alternatives? This is something we need to think about carefully because it could solve many of the other issues we face.

Perhaps, rather than having a world in which there is intense rivalry and competition, we need a world more like that suggested by George. We need one that is in tune with nature. A world where there is a sharing of ideas, technology and cultures, in an enlightened way; a world that allows us to feel a sense of community.

Whatever, we need to rethink how we are governed.

6. *We need to have fewer babies*

Finally, we need to control the population. In the great debate about the number of people on the planet, an underlying truth is often left unsaid; population growth on Earth *must* at some point cease.

Unless we take steps to control the number of people, the damaging effects on the world's resources will continue to worsen until we realize there are limits to what we can achieve, or we are confronted by a catastrophe large enough to turn us around. Logically then, it makes sense for us to reduce our birth rates in humane ways rather than waiting for death rates to solve the problem for us.

As the developing world tries to adopt the consumption patterns of the West, the pressure for change will grow. Yet, instead of managing this problem responsibly, the West is still offering developing countries a prize they cannot win. Modern economics has sold all of us a dream of progress, freedom and wealth. But this will be impossible for most people in the world to achieve. It is a cruel hoax fed by wrong-headed modern economists and those who hope to profit along the way.

There are limits to growth and many of them are determined by the number of people on the planet. As long as the world's population keeps growing, the sooner the crunch point will come.

A solution to this problem is hard to see. At the very least, we need to bring in universal birth control and ban the activities of many religious groups.

All they do is encourage even more people to believe in a dream that cannot come true.

Endnote

1. Edward Abbey, *One Life at a Time, Please* (New York: Henry Holt, 1988), p. 21.

15

YOU. YOU HAVE A ROLE NOW TOO

To feel much for others and little for ourselves, to indulge our benevolent affections, constitutes the perfection of human nature.

Adam Smith, *The Theory of Moral Sentiments*

Faced with such enormous problems these suggestions are obviously only a small part of the solution. To address the challenges we face will need global cooperation, consensus and leadership.

It will need your participation too.

We all have a responsibility for where humanity stands and for where it is going. It makes no sense for us to complain about inequality, about the world's resources being squandered, and about the fate that awaits our grandchildren, without responding.

We can start by becoming less accepting. In the West and Japan everyone should have been more skeptical about the modern economic model we were sold, with its promises of growth fueled by consumption and debt. In Japan everyone could see the buildup of debt was not sustainable yet no one had the courage to do anything about it. In much of the developing world, it has become clear that the hoped-for pace of economic development cannot continue. We are on a road to nowhere. Yet few have the courage to say so.

Those living in the US and much of Europe should have seen the flaws in their economic systems too. Any model of progress that offered so much reward, to so few, so quickly, could not be functioning properly, or it would run counter to economic history, to the pace of development that naturally exists. Did we all really think that we had found a better way, when hundreds of generations during past millennia had not? We all knew that there was some sleight of hand going on, a piece of smooth-talking political and economic trickery.

Yet most people ignored what their heads were telling them, while their wallets and waists grew fatter. Western citizens should have questioned a system that demands people give up their historic loyalties to places and communities, that seemed to shrug off widespread frauds and injustices, and that led to massive inequalities and social divisions. They should have seen the emptiness of their purpose. They should have seen that denying millions of people access to healthcare, denying workers the right to organize themselves and a system that allowed a small group to become multi-millionaires through the destruction of nature, was wrong.

We all believed that growth was good, that it was a valid measure of human progress. We believed that unregulated free-markets were the most efficient way to allocate society's resources. We believed that globalization was advantageous, despite the unequal way in which the benefits accrued. We believed that big businesses and big banks would behave benevolently, and in our interests, just as long as they were free from government interference.

As well as blaming ourselves for our foolishness, we should blame the economists for their sloppy thinking and the politicians for selling us such nonsense. As Edward Abbey said, "economics, no matter how econometric it pretends to be, resembles meteorology more than mathematics. [It is] a cloudy science of swirling vapors, signifying nothing."[1]

We put our faith in this pseudoscience, in these ethereal vapors.

Our belief in these wrong-headed ideas has allowed economic power and wealth to become concentrated in the hands of a few powerful people, institutions and businesses. We have sat back and watched, while a small minority have consumed far more than their rightful share of the world's resources to gain far more than their rightful share of the world's wealth. We have allowed them to exploit the planet beyond its tolerances, exhausting our reserves and the resources upon which our lives depend.

At the very least, we all need to become more skeptical about what politicians and economists tell us.

We also need to ask ourselves what life is about. It is not about consuming, about money and about growth. There are a vast array of other pursuits that can fulfill us—social, cultural, intellectual and spiritual pursuits—which do not drain the planet of its resources. We each need to ask ourselves what it is that we want. We need to take control of our future, to create just and sustainable societies. Everyone acting in their own interests, without harming others, just as Smith believed, is a good place to start.

We will also need a sense of optimism. In many ways humanity is sitting in a cave, facing the back wall. Everything is dark. We cannot see a way forward. But there is a way to go, there is a way out. We can change the future if we wish, if we turn around.

In the end, achieving a different means of social progress is about you and me. It is about your ideas and mine. It is about what we can do to change our model of social development. It is about what we can do to change our approach to economics. It is about how we can create a system that is less concerned with maximizing selfish gains. It is about how we can take a different approach to resource use, to end the senseless exploitation of our planet for short-term profit. It is about how we can put new efforts into innovation, create political reform and improve our societies to create a more sustainable future.

We need to develop an economic model for the future that is not held captive by the free market, by consumption and by growth for its own sake. We need to think differently about inequality, poverty and population. We need to think about how we can restore the bonds of community. We need not abandon free market economics entirely—but we need to ensure that is managed to meet our needs—all of our needs. For too long it has served the needs of a few. It has lost sight of its origins, abandoned those "moral sentiments." It needs to have rules that ensure sustainability, equality, justice and fairness.

Our societies should be ruled by us, not by the market.

> A wise man does not look upon himself as a whole, separated and detached from every other part of nature. He considers himself as an atom, a particle, of an immense and infinite system.[2]
>
> ADAM SMITH

Endnotes

1. Edward Abbey, *One Life at a Time, Please, A San Francisco Journey (Day 6),* (New York: Henry Holt, 1988).
2. Adam Smith, *The Theory of Moral Sentiments* VII.II.24 (London: A. Millar, 1790), 6th Edition, First published in London, 1759.

INDEX